California DMV Exam Workbook

400+ Driving Test Questions and Answers to Pass the Exam at Your First Attempt

By

Gordon Chambers

© Copyright 2023 by Gordon Chambers - All rights reserved.

This document is geared towards providing exact and reliable information in regard to the topic and issue covered. The publication is sold with the idea that the publisher is not required to render accounting, officially permitted, or otherwise, qualified services. If advice is necessary, legal, or professional, a practiced individual in the profession should be ordered.

- From a Declaration of Principles, which was accepted and approved equally by a Committee of the American Bar Association and a Committee of Publishers and Associations? In no way is it legal to reproduce, duplicate, or transmit any part of this document in either electronic means or in printed format. Recording of this publication is strictly prohibited, and any storage of this document is not allowed unless with written permission from the publisher. All rights reserved. The information provided herein is stated to be truthful and consistent, in that any liability, in terms of inattention or otherwise, by any usage or abuse of any policies, processes, or directions contained within is the solitary and utter responsibility of the recipient reader. Under no circumstances will any legal responsibility or blame be held against the publisher for any reparation, damages, or monetary loss due to the information herein, either directly or indirectly. Respective authors own all copyrights not held by the publisher. The information herein is offered for informational purposes solely and is universal as so. The presentation of the information is without contract or any type of guarantee assurance. The trademarks that are used are without any consent, and the publication of the trademark is without permission or backing by the trademark owner. All trademarks and brands within this book are for clarifying purposes only and are owned by the owners themselves, not affiliated with this document.

Contents

Introduction 5
Chapter 1: All you need to know about The California Driver's License 7
    1.1 Acquiring a Learner's Permit and a Driver's License 7
    1.2 Card Classifications 9
    1.3 The Examination Process 10
    1.4 Driver's License Replacement, Upgrade, and Renewal Procedures 12
Chapter 2: Driving Fundamentals: An Introduction 14
    2.1 Signaling, Audible Warnings, and Lighting Systems 14
    2.2 Vehicle Control Techniques 17
    2.3 Road Navigation Techniques 17
Chapter 3: Laws and Traffic Regulations 33
    3.1 Traffic Management 33
    3.2 Traffic Signals 33
    3.3 Pedestrian Signals or Signs 34
    3.4 Signs 35
    3.5 Railroad crossing signals and signs 38
    3.6 Construction and Maintenance Traffic Control Signs 39
    3.7 Guidelines for Right-of-Way: Who Moves First? 40
    3.8 Intersections 40
    3.9 Roundabouts 41
    3.10 Pedestrians 41
    3.11 Crosswalks 41
    3.12 Braking 42
    3.13 Missing Spots (the No Zone) 42
    3.14 Turning 42
    3.15 Maneuvering 42
    3.16 Work Zones and Road Workers 43
    3.17 Vehicles Carrying Dangerous Loads 43
Chapter 4: California DMV Permit Practice Test 1 (50) 44
Chapter 5: California DMV Permit Practice Test 2 (50) 52
Chapter 6: California DMV Permit Practice Test 3 (50) 60
Chapter 7: California DMV Permit Practice Test 4 (50) 68
Chapter 8: California DMV Permit Practice Test 5 (50) 77
Chapter 9: California DMV Permit Practice Test 6 (50) 85

Chapter 10: California DMV Permit Practice Test 7 (50) 93
Chapter 11: California DMV Permit Practice Test 8 (50) 102
Conclusion.. 112

Introduction

Would you like your California driver's licence as quickly as possible? In Florida, obtaining a driver's licence is straightforward. Everything you need to know to prepare for the exam, gather the required documentation, and pass the knowledge test and driving test. You can obtain all the knowledge required to apply for a Florida driver's licence with the help of our comprehensive guide.

The Florida Highway Safety and Motor Vehicle Administration (FLHSMV) is mandated by law to collect specific information from drivers licence applicants. This data is used for a variety of purposes, including population monitoring, ensuring that roads are safe for transportation, monitoring financial activities, and upholding the law. The issuance of a driver's licence or identification card is contingent upon submitting the required information.

Unless expressly precluded, documents produced or received by DPS in the course of official business are subject to examination under California law. Your identification, including your name, address, and driver's licence number, will not be disclosed without your consent. We reserve the right, if necessary, to share your information with law enforcement and other entities. Your Social Security number, medical information, and emergency contact information are not disclosed unless mandated by law.

In order to obtain a driver's licence, you must demonstrate adequate vision and hearing. If you need corrective lenses (glasses or contacts) or a hearing aid to pass the test, you will be issued a driver's licence with restrictions. This licence requires you to carry these items while operating a motor vehicle at all times.

In order to obtain a driver's licence in the state, you must also pass the Class E Knowledge Exam. If you previously passed the permit examination, you are considered to have fulfilled this requirement.

In addition to your defensive driving skills, you will be examined on your knowledge of California's traffic laws and regulations. This type of exam is commonly referred to as a "written exam," which is merely another term for it. As this is a multiple-choice examination, however, no writing is required. To pass the exam, you must correctly respond to at least 40 of the fifty questions.

California drivers must pass the Class E Driving Skills Test, also known as the California Driving Test, in order to obtain a licence. This test must be taken while operating a motor vehicle in a DPS-approved location.

A visit can be scheduled using the Online Appointment Service and Information System. Before you can take the test, you must drive a legally insured and licenced vehicle to the testing location. You will be permitted to take the driver's examination if your vehicle passes the safety inspection.

This book will help you pass the California DMV Exam. Receive a copy immediately, as it contains sample questions and other information necessary for obtaining your licence.

Chapter 1: All you need to know about The California Driver's License

In California, a legitimate driver's licence is required to operate a motor vehicle, permitting drivers to legally and safely navigate public roads. In California, prospective drivers must pass both the written and driving skills exams in order to obtain a driving licence. The purpose of these tests is to evaluate a candidate's knowledge of the rules, regulations, and best practises outlined in this manual. It is necessary to obtain the licence class that corresponds to the vehicle type being driven. Class C noncommercial driver's licences are adequate for the preponderance of vehicles. Nevertheless, certain vehicles, such as motorcycles, commercial vehicles, and specialised automobiles, require a specialised licence class. By obtaining the necessary licence and adhering to the specified guidelines, individuals can confidently and lawfully operate a variety of vehicles on California's public roads.

1.1 Acquiring a Learner's Permit and a Driver's License

If you do not possess a legitimate driving licence from California or another state, you must apply for a learner's permit prior to taking the driving test.

What you require

When applying for a learner's permit or driver's license in California, you will need to provide:

• Proof of California residency, such as a utility bill showing your name and address. Some exceptions may apply.

• Identification documents showing your full legal name and date of birth.

• Your Social Security number. Exceptions may be available for some applicants.

• Documents proving your legal name if the name on your identification does not match the name on your application.

Acquiring an Instructional Permit

To submit a Class C instruction permits application:

- Fill out an application for an ID card and driver's license.
- Submit your paperwork.

- Pay an application fee that is not refundable.
- Pass your test of knowledge (s).
- Pass the eye exam.

Also, if you are under 18, you must:

You must bring certain documents when applying for a learner's permit or driver's license:

Proof of residency in California: You need to show 2 documents with your name and California address, like a utility bill or lease agreement. Exceptions may apply.

Identification: You need to show official ID with your full legal name and date of birth like a passport or birth certificate.

Social Security number: You must provide your Social Security number. Exceptions are available for some applicants.

Legal name change documents: If the name on your ID doesn't match the application, you need documents proving your legal name change, like a marriage certificate or court order.

Driving Schools and Education

A number of secondary schools and driving academies with DMV licences provide driver education and training. Instructors must possess a valid teacher identification certificate. Request to examine it. For more information on selecting a driving school, visit the website and select the Driver Training Schools page.

Getting the Driving License

To obtain a driver's licence after obtaining an instruction permit, you must: • Drive with a licenced Californian who is at least 18 years old (25 years old for juveniles) and who is at least 18 years old. This individual must be seated close to the steering wheel to assume control in an emergency.

Also, if you are under 18, you must:

• Prior to scheduling your behind-the-wheel driving test, you must: • Have had a California or other state-issued instruction permit for at least 6 months (or until you are 18), whichever comes first.

- Practise driving for at least 50 hours with a licenced California driver who is at least 25 years old. There must be a ten-hour sleep period.

- Be at least 16 years old.

- Attest to successfully completing both driver education and training programmes.

Minors: Restrictions and Exemptions

Provisional will be printed on your driver's licence if you are under 18 years old. As a provisional driver, the following are prohibited:

- With anyone under the age of 20, unless accompanied by a parent, legal guardian, or motorist who is at least 25 years old and has a valid California driver's licence.

- Between 5 a.m. and 11 p.m. during the first year after obtaining a licence. • For vehicles operated or used for rental that require a business Class A, B, or C licence.

These restrictions do not apply if you: • Have a medical necessity and are unable to locate an alternative mode of transportation that is reasonable. You must bring a memo signed by your physician. The note must state your medical condition and the anticipated date of recovery.

- Drive to class or an academic function. It would be helpful to have a note from your school's principal, dean, or designated representative. • A family member must drive the vehicle. A note from a parent or legal guardian must be carried at all times. The note must include the family member's name, the reason you must travel, and the expected completion time.

- Transportation to and from employment is required. You must carry a memo that must be signed by your supervisor. Your employment verification must be included in the correspondence.

1.2 Card Classifications

Driver's License with Real ID Compliance

Starting from May 2025, it is mandatory for your ID card or driver's license to be REAL ID compatible if you intend to use it for the following purposes:

- Participating in federal programs
- Entering federal facilities
- Boarding domestic flights within the United States

Driving Authorization for Undocumented Residents

Regardless of immigration status, California residents can obtain driver's licenses.

Identification Documents

Anyone who meets the requirements may get an ID card to use as identification. Simply stated, you cannot drive there. You will need to provide identification, evidence of residence, and your social security number in order to get an ID. Visit the official website to apply for a California driver's licence or identity card and to get the most recent details on the acceptable forms of identification, the costs, and any applicable discounts.

1.3 The Examination Process

Below is a summary of the tests for a driver's license:

Skills Assessment

You must pass a knowledge test with multiple-choice questions in order to apply for an original driver's licence. You have three chances to pass before you need to reapply. After failing a knowledge test, a minor has seven days (not including the day of failure) to retake it.

Visual Assessment

The vision test is an important part of obtaining a driver's license. The DMV ensures applicants have adequate vision to safely drive.

If you wear glasses or contact lenses and pass the vision test with them, your license will require you to wear them while driving.

If you fail the vision test, your eye doctor must complete a Certificate of Vision Assessment. This form certifies you have the minimum vision needed to drive safely. You submit this form to the DMV to obtain a restricted license.

Check official DMV websites for more details regarding vision requirements and procedures for obtaining a restricted license due to vision impairment. Accurate information on vision test requirements is crucial for obtaining an appropriate driver's license.

Behind-the-Wheel Evaluation

Vision is critical for safe driving. The DMV vision test ensures applicants have adequate vision to obtain a license.

If you require corrective lenses and pass with them, your license will specify you must wear them while driving.

If you fail the test, your eye doctor must fill out a Certificate of Vision Assessment. This certifies you have minimum vision to drive safely with restrictions. You submit it to obtain a restricted license.

Check the official DMV website for details on:

- Vision requirements
- Restricted license procedures
- Needed documents
- Vision test instructions

Accurate information is vital for obtaining the appropriate license based on your vision. The DMV website is the definitive source.

Pre-Test Information Required by DMV Examiner

• **Windscreen** - The windscreen must be completely and visibly visible to both the driver and the DMV inspector. Cracks in the windscreen could cause your exam to be delayed.

• There must be a minimum of two rearview mirrors. One must be located on the left side of your vehicle.

• **Horn:** Specifically designed for the vehicle, in functional condition, and audible from at least 200 feet away.

• All occupants must fasten their seat belts appropriately and at all times while in the vehicle.

• **Driver window** - The driver's side window must be opened.

• The left and right brake lamps must be operational.

• **Foot brake:** When the brake pedal is engaged, there must be at least an inch of space between the bottom of the pedal and the floorboard.

• Turn/arm indicators; left/right turns; slowed or halted motion

- Windscreen wipers: control arm or switch - you may be required to provide evidence that they work.

- Tyres must have a consistent tread depth of at least 0.3 millimetres. A driving examination does not permit the use of doughnut-shaped tyres.

- How to apply and disengage the parking brake in an emergency

Supplementary Details for Your Behind-the-Wheel Examination

The driving test evaluates your ability to handle various road and traffic conditions, not how advanced the vehicle's technology is.

During the test:

Do not rely on driver assistance systems like automatic lane changes, lane keep assist or adaptive cruise control. These cannot be used to pass the test.

Avoid using technology like rear cameras and blind spot monitors instead of checking mirrors and doing shoulder checks. Technology supplements good driving habits but cannot replace them.

The purpose of the test is to ensure you can drive safely using good habits, proper vehicle inspection and visual awareness - not advanced automotive technology. Even the most modern vehicles with the latest safety features require a professional driver who follows all rules of the road.

Focus on skills like:

Checking mirrors and blind spots

Maintaining proper speed and distance from other vehicles

Using signals and lane positioning correctly

Visually confirming no obstacles before turning or changing lanes.

Driver assistance technologies are meant to aid - not replace - a driver's vision, judgement and control of the vehicle.

1.4 Driver's License Replacement, Upgrade, and Renewal Procedures

- You can update name and gender information online at the DMV website.

- After moving, get a replacement license for a fee. Driving with a suspended license is illegal.
- Notify the DMV of your new address within 10 days of moving. Ensure your correct mailing address is on file.
- The DMV may require additional ID to issue a license. Bring valid ID if your current license and ID expire on the same day.
- Minors need a parent or guardian's approval to apply. Your old license is invalid after getting a new one, so destroy it.
- If you live outside California and cannot renew your license, you may request a one-year extension.
- Main points:
- Update name, gender and address online or in-person
- Get a replacement license after moving, for a fee
- Notify DMV within 10 days of moving
- Bring additional valid ID if both license and ID expire on the same day
- Minors need parental approval
- Destroy old licenses after getting a new one
- Non-residents may request a 1-year extension if unable to renew in-person
- Ensure your information is accurate and up-to-date with the DMV to drive legally in California.

Chapter 2: Driving Fundamentals: An Introduction

- You're driving may be impacted by your health.
- Seeing threats in varying lighting situations, judging distances, adjusting traffic speed, and reading road signs all need vision.
- Drowsiness and fatigue may impair your eyesight and increase the amount of time it takes you to respond to risks.
- Being physically and mentally aware is necessary to make the best decision in any traffic situation, particularly an unplanned one.
- Medication: Both prescription and over-the-counter medications might make it difficult for you to drive. Numerous drugs may help people fall asleep. You need to be mindful of the effects of your medicines.
- Hearing: You need to be able to hear horns, sirens, motorcycles, or screaming tyres in order to be aware of possible risks. It is not permitted to drive while using earphones or a headset.
- Health: Your doctor is required to inform the DMV if they feel you have a medical condition, such as conscious lapses, that might make it unsafe for you to drive. Patients who are at least 14 years old are subject to this rule.ha

2.1 Signaling, Audible Warnings, and Lighting Systems

It's crucial to use your headlights, horn, and signals to signal to other motorists, pedestrians, and bicycles.

Proper Signaling Techniques

Always signal your intentions to other road users when:

- Turning
- Changing lanes
- Accelerating from a stop
- Slowing down or stopping

How to signal:

Car drivers: use your turn signal lights. Always activate your signal at least 100 feet before turning or changing lanes.

Motorcycle riders: extend your arm straight out to indicate the direction you will turn or change lanes. Keep your arm extended until the maneuver is completed.

Bicycle riders: point your arm straight out in the direction you will turn. Keep your arm extended during the entire turn.

Signaling is essential to communicate your intentions and allow others time to react. Not signaling can lead to collisions. Use proper signals consistently to drive safely and courteously.

Key points:

- Always signal before turning, changing lanes, accelerating or stopping
- Car drivers should use turn signals
- Motorcyclists extend the arm straight out
- Cyclists point the arm in the direction of the turn
- Keep signaling until the maneuver is complete
- Proper signaling communication is vital for traffic to flow smoothly and safely.

Effective Use of the Horn

Use your car's horn to alert other drivers to your presence or to a hazard. How to use your horn

1. On winding mountain roads where you can't see more than 200 feet in front of you, be aware of oncoming vehicles.
2. Prevent colliding.

Headlight Usage Guidelines

Use your headlights:

• When visibility is less than 1000 feet due to conditions like rain, fog, snow, dust, smoke, etc.

• At dawn, dusk and nighttime - at least an hour before sunset to an hour after sunrise.

• When required by traffic signs or laws.

• When the sun is low - traveling towards the rising or setting sun.

• Do not drive with parking lights only - use low beam headlights.

- In tunnels and on mountain roads during the day.

Specifically:

- Within 500 feet of an oncoming vehicle, switch to low beams from high beams.
- Within 300 feet of a vehicle you're following, use low beams.

Headlights make your vehicle more visible to others and help you see the road ahead - especially in poor visibility conditions. Use them whenever visibility is reduced to ensure safety.

Key points:

- Use headlights in conditions with reduced visibility - rain, snow, fog, dawn/dusk, etc.
- Obey traffic sign and legal requirements for headlights
- Avoid high beams within 300-500 feet of other vehicles
- Never drive with parking lights only - use low beam headlights at minimum

Proper headlight usage increases your vehicle's visibility and helps prevent collisions in low light conditions.

Utilizing Emergency Flashers Safely

Use the following techniques to alert drivers behind you if you may spot an accident or danger up ahead:

1. Three or four light taps on the brake pedal.
2. Set your emergency flashers to on.
3. When braking and slowing down, use a hand gesture.

If your car needs to halt due to trouble:

1. If at all feasible, pull over far from any oncoming vehicles.
2. Set your emergency flashers to on. Use your turn signals if your car doesn't have emergency flashers.
3. If you can't get off the road, pull over such oncoming traffic can see you and your car from behind.
4. Never stop just after cresting a hill or going around a curve. It's possible that other motorists won't spot your car in time to avert a collision.

5. If you can't get off the road, pull over such oncoming traffic can see you and your car from behind.
6. Make an emergency roadside assistance call, then remain in your car until aid arrives.

2.2 Vehicle Control Techniques

It's crucial to drive with both hands on the wheel whenever possible in order to handle your vehicle.

Hand-to-Hand Steering

Using this steering-wheel technique

1. Start by positioning your hands at 9 and 3 or 8 and 4.

2. Refrain from crossing your hands over the middle of the steering wheel.

3. Maintain this position at all times, even while turning.

Proper Technique: Hand-Over-Hand Steering

Employ this steering-wheel technique when you need to park, turn slowly, or recover from a skid. To apply this approach:

1. Place your hands at 8 and 4 o'clock to begin.
2. Grab the opposite side of the steering wheel by crossing it.
3. Release your other hand off the steering wheel.
4. Grab the wheel with the arm that is still holding it and pull yourself up.

Steering with a Single Hand

There are just two circumstances in which one-handed steering may be necessary:

1. While using car controls that call you to take your hand off the steering wheel.
2. When you turn while backing up, check your rearward direction. Put your hand on the steering wheel at the noon position.

2.3 Road Navigation Techniques

Understanding Traffic Lane Systems

A piece of road designated for one line of traffic is called a traffic lane.

Yellow Line: Maintaining Uninterrupted Traffic Flow

Do not cross double yellow lines except for:

• Making a legal U-turn crossing a single set of lines.

• Entering a driveway by making a left turn across a single set of lines.

• Entering an HOV lane that has a dedicated entrance on the left.

A double double yellow lines barrier:

• Consists of two sets of lines separated by 2 feet or more.

• Cannot be driven or turned on, over, left or right except at defined openings.

You may cross double lines to:

• Drive on the opposite side of the road when your side is closed for construction or other reasons as indicated by signs.

Key points:

• Do not cross double yellow lines unless permitted to do so legally

• Exceptions include U-turns, entering driveways or HOV lanes

• A double double yellow lines barrier cannot be crossed except at openings

• You may cross double lines if directed by signs due to road closure

Follow the rules regarding double yellow lines to drive legally and avoid collisions. Only cross them in permitted situations to ensure safety.

Flawed Yellow Line: Addressing Traffic Line Deficiencies

If a yellow line is broken adjacent to your driving lane, it means you can pass. Pass only when it is secure.

Dual Solid White Lines: Navigating the Significance of Double Lane Dividers in California

A lane barrier between regular use and a preferred usage lane, such as a carpool (HOV) lane, is indicated by two solid double-white lines. Moreover, multiple solid white lines could be in or close to the motorway on- and off-ramps. Never cross double solid white lines when changing lanes. As soon as you spot a single, broken white line, stop.

Singular White Line: Enhancing Roadway Clarity and Safety

- The same-direction traffic lanes are identified by a single solid white line. This also applies to one-way streets

Recognizing and Addressing Faded Lane Markings

On roads with two or more lanes in one direction, broken white lines divide the traffic lanes.

Yield Chart: Navigating Right-of-Way Responsibilities on California Roads

A yield line is a continuous white line with triangles that directs oncoming traffic to stop or yield. The triangles indicate the direction of incoming cars.

Final Stretch Lane Markings: Ensuring Clear Direction and Safe Navigation

Large broken lines are typically used to indicate the end of the street and motorway lanes. Be ready to exit the motorway or for the lane to end if you drive in a lane with broken lines. Search for a sign directing you to merge or exit.

Lane Selection

Numerology is frequently used to refer to traffic lanes. The Number 1 Lane is the leftmost (or fastest) lane. The Number 2 Lane is the lane that is located to the right of the Number 1 Lane. Next comes the third lane, etc.

Here are a few pointers for selecting a lane.

- When entering or leaving traffic, use the right lane.
- When passing or turning left, use the left lane.

Types of Lanes

The key points regarding passing lanes and HOV lanes in California are:

Passing Lanes:

- The leftmost lane is used for passing slower vehicles.
- Only pass when it is safe to do so. Use turn signals and check blind spots before changing lanes.
- HOV Lanes:

Designated for low emission vehicles, carpools, motorcycles and buses to reduce traffic.

To use an HOV lane you must:

- Have a low emission vehicle with DMV decal
- Have the minimum number of occupants indicated by signs
- Be a motorcycle rider (unless posted otherwise)
- HOV lanes are marked with:
- "Carpool Lane" text and diamond emblem on the road
- Signs showing hours of operation and minimum occupants required
- Enter and exit HOV lanes only at designated locations:
- Do not cross double solid lines except at openings

Key rules:

- The left lane is for passing only
- Pass only when safe
- Meet the posted vehicle/occupant requirements to use an HOV lane
- Enter and exit HOV lanes at designated points only
- Following these rules for passing lanes and HOV lanes helps promote safe and efficient driving on California highways.

Lane Changes

Before a lane change:

- Message.
- Verify your reflections.
- To ensure the lane is clear, look behind you in the direction you intend to move.
- Scan the traffic in front of and behind you.
- Check to see if the next lane has room for your car. Before a lane change, you do not have to slow down.

As often as you can, stay in one lane. Avoid darting in and out of the traffic.

Accident risk may be increased by sudden lane or direction changes.

Continue travelling after beginning to cross an intersection. If you begin to turn, finish the turn. When you miss a turn, keep going until you can turn around safely and legally.

Center-Left Turn Lanes

• A centre left turn lane is marked by:

Two painted lines, a solid outer line and a broken inner line

"Left Turn Only" signs

• It is for preparing for and making left turns and U-turns, not for through traffic or passing.

• Only travel up to 200 feet in the centre left turn lane before making a left turn.

• Be cautious of other vehicles in the centre left turn lane approaching from behind.

• Check your blind spots and mirror before merging into the centre left turn lane.

• Only turn left when it is clear and safe to do so.

• Merge completely into the centre left turn lane to allow traffic to pass on either side.

• Do not obstruct through traffic while waiting in the centre left turn lane.

Main ideas:

• Centre left turn lanes are for left turns and U-turns only, not through traffic.

• Only travel a short distance in the lane before turning.

• Check carefully for oncoming traffic in the lane before merging.

• Wait fully in the lane to avoid obstructing traffic behind you.

By understanding and following the rules of centre left turn lanes, you can turn left safely and courteously on multi-lane roads.

Bicycle Lanes: Supporting Safe and Sustainable Cycling Infrastructure in California

Only cyclists are allowed in bicycle lanes, which run alongside car traffic. Often, a single, solid white line or markers are used to identify them. To make them more visible, they are occasionally painted a brilliant green.

Driving inside a bicycle lane is prohibited unless you are:

- Rotating (within 200 feet of an intersection).
- Getting on or off the road.
- Placement (where permitted).

There are various kinds of bike lanes and markers, including:

- Bicycle markings on shared roadways: These markings warn motorists that cyclists can occupy the lane and assist riders in maintaining a safe lane position in traffic.
- Bicyclists may only use a separate bikeway, which is physically isolated from motor vehicle traffic. They are also referred to as protected bike lanes or cycle tracks. Flexible posts, grade separation, rigid barriers, or on-street parking are some examples of the separation.
- Bicycle boulevard: Gives priority to bicycling on roads where vehicles also travel.
- Bike lanes: They have been installed on streets with heavy traffic. Usually denoted by a single, solid white line that becomes a dashed line when it approaches an intersection.
- Buffered bike lane: This bike lane uses chevrons or diagonal markers to create more space between it and on-street parking and traffic.
- Bike route: On streets with shared vehicular and bicycle traffic, bike route signs and shared road markings indicate a preferred route for bicycles.

Lanes and Turnout Zones: Utilizing Dedicated Spaces for Safe Stopping and Turning

There are designated turnout sections or lanes on several two-lane roadways. To make room for vehicles following you to pass, merge into these regions or lanes. When you are going slow on a two-lane road when passing is risky, and there are 5 or more vehicles following you, you must utilise a turnout zone or lane to let other vehicles pass.

Executing Turns: Mastering the Art of Safe and Precise Maneuvering

<u>Right Turns</u>

To make a right turn:

- Keep your vehicle close to the road's right edge. Enter at the entrance if a dedicated right turn lane is available. Between 200 feet of the turn, you are allowed to drive in the bike lane. Verify your blind areas for bicycles.
- Reduce your speed and glance over your right shoulder.
- Remain behind the boundary line. A limit line, which is a broad white line indicating where and how to stop before such an intersection or crosswalk, is visible to traffic. If there isn't a limit line, pause before you cross the street. In the absence of a crosswalk, pause before approaching the crossing.
- Keep an eye out for people walking, bicycling, or riding motorcycles between your car and the curb.
- Start flashing the turn signal about 100 feet in advance.
- If it's safe to turn, look in both directions (left, right, left).
- Finish turning in the right-hand lane. Never make a wide turn into another lane.

Understanding California's Regulations and Safety Considerations for Right Turns on Red

After coming to a complete stop, you may turn right at a red light unless a No Turn on Red sign is present. For right turns, follow the same procedures outlined previously.

Turn Right Against Red Arrows

At a red arrow signal, it is prohibited to turn right. If the light is red, do not turn until it turns green.

Right Turns in the Bus Lanes of Public Transportation

It is prohibited to drive, halt, park, or leave a vehicle in an area designated for public transportation buses. Signs will indicate that the lanes are reserved for bus use only. To make a right turn, you may cross a bus lane, however.

Dedicated Right Turn Lanes:

If a designated right-turn lane does not merge into another lane, you may make a right turn without halting. Even if the light is red for vehicles proceeding directly through the intersection, you may still make your turn. On the right verge of the right turn lane, you must obey any traffic signals or signs. Always yield to pedestrians in crosswalks when turning.

Left Turns

To turn left:

- Drive into the left turn lane or close to the center divider.
- Within 200 feet of the turn, move into a two-way center left turn lane.
- Respect any vehicles, cyclists, or motorcycles already using the lane. Always move aside for pedestrians.
- At the opening, move into the allocated left turn lane. Avoid crossing any boundaries.
- One hundred feet before the turn, start signaling.
- Remain behind the boundary line. If there isn't a limit line, pause before you cross the street. In the absence of a crosswalk, pause before approaching the crossing.
- When it is safe to start your turn, look in both directions (left-right-left).
- Make your turn in the left lane and continue into the junction.
- Avoid making a sudden turn in the direction of incoming traffic.
- Keep your wheels facing straight ahead until it is safe to begin your turn. If a car hits you from behind while your wheels are oriented to the left, you risk being thrown into the path of oncoming traffic.
- Smoothly pick up speed prior to and following the turn.
- In the new lane, let the steering wheel straighten.

<u>Left Turns Against Red Arrows</u>

While transferring from a one-way street to another one, you are permitted to turn left against a red light. Verify that there are no signs blocking the turn. When there is a green light, give way to other vehicles, pedestrians, and cyclists. When it is safe to turn, look both ways.

U-turns: Navigating California's Regulations and Safety Guideline

Turning your car around to head back in the direction you came from is known as a U-turn. Use the left turn lane or the far-left lane when signaling your U-turn. You could perform a U-turn:

- During a green signal or green arrow at an intersection, unless a no-turn sign is posted.
- Between two double yellow lines.
- If no cars are within 200 feet of you in a residential area.

Never U-turn:

- In business districts are the areas of a city or town where most offices and establishments are located.
- On a one-way roadway;
- Where there is a No U-turn sign.
- Near a railroad crossing or nearby.
- Outside of a firehouse. Never make a U-turn in a fire station driveway.

Variety of Turns: Illustrating Diverse Maneuvers at Road Intersections

The descriptions below pertain to the number next to the cars in the pictures. Keep an eye out for bicycles, motorbikes, and pedestrians between your car and the curb. There may be arrows or signage that let you know you can turn from or terminate in more than one lane when making turns.

<u>Right Turns: Executing Safe and Efficient Maneuvers from Two-Way Streets</u>

Start and finish the turn in the lane most near the right side of the road. Never swerve wide into a different lane of traffic.

<u>Left Turns from Two-Way Streets: Safely Navigating Intersection Transitions</u>

Start making the turn in the left lane that is nearest to the centre of the road. End the turn in the left lane closest to the centre of the roadway, moving in the direction of your car to lower the likelihood of a collision.

<u>Turning Left onto Two-Way Streets: Safe and Smooth Maneuvers from One-Way Roads</u>

Start the turn from the far-left lane. End the turn in the left lane closest to the centre of the roadway moving in the direction of your car to lower the likelihood of a collision.

<u>Turning Left onto One-Way Streets: Safely Transitioning from Two-Way Roads</u>

Beginning in the lane closest to the middle of the roadway (far-left lane). If there are 3 or more lanes available in the direction you're travelling, you can finish your turn in any of them.

<u>Left Turns between One-Way Streets: Navigating Safe and Efficient Maneuvers</u>

It is recommended to initiate the maneuver from the far left most lane. To make a left turn, cyclists are permitted to utilize the lane designated for that purpose. You can complete your turn in any available lane provided there are three or maybe more lanes going in the direction you're turning.

<u>Right Turns between One-Way Streets: Safely Transitioning and Navigating Intersection changes</u>

In the far right lane, begin the turn. When it's safe, you can finish the turn in any lane.

<u>One-Way to Two-Way: Negotiating Safe Turns at "T" Intersections</u>

The right-of-way is given to vehicles travelling straight through the intersection.

From the center lane, you can turn either right or left.

Braking Techniques: Mastering Safe and Effective Deceleration on the Road

Here are the key points regarding stopping and merging onto highways:

- When stopping:
- Do not stop past the limit line or crosswalk.
- Leave enough space to see the rear wheels of the vehicle in front of you.
- Remove your foot from the accelerator and apply light brake pressure to slow down smoothly.
- Ensure you have enough room and time to stop safely.

Merging onto highways:

- Yield to through traffic already on the highway.
- Stay in the correct on-ramp lane.
- Use turn signals and mirror checks.
- Match the highway speed or merge at a speed close to traffic.
- Maintain a 3 second following distance.

- Check behind you before changing lanes or merging.
- Merge into a gap that is large enough for your vehicle.
- Merge into traffic when it is safe to do so. Keep moving if no gaps are available.
- Signal and change lanes one at a time if merging across multiple lanes.
- Always check your blind spots for vehicles.

Main ideas:

- Stop smoothly behind the limit line, leaving space to see rear wheels of the front vehicle.
- Yield and match speeds when merging onto highways. Signal and change lanes one at a time.
- Check mirrors, blind spots and over your shoulder before merging or changing lanes.
- Being aware of how to properly stop and merge helps you enter highways safely and seamlessly.

How to safely leave a highway:

- If you intend to change lanes, make each shift slowly. To verify your blind spots, signal and turn around.
- While in the appropriate lane, give five seconds' notice (or around 400 feet) before exiting.
- Before leaving, be sure to move at a safe speed and avoid crossing any solid lines.

Pedestrian Safety: Guidelines for Entering and Crossing the Street Safely

When reentering traffic after a complete stop, indicate and allow ample room to pick up speed. You require a space that is: to combine, enters, or exit traffic.

- A full block on the road, or roughly 300 feet.
- On city streets, half a block is equivalent to 150 feet.
- If people or cars are in your way while you have a green signal, do not begin crossing the intersection.

Never presume that an approaching car with its right turn signal on is turning before it gets to you when making a left turn. The car might have accidentally turned on its signal or be preparing to turn immediately past you. Before starting the left turn, could you wait for the car to start its turn?

Exercising Caution: Understanding When to Avoid Passing on the Road:

- Within 100 feet of a railroad crossing, bridge, tunnel, or other dangerous place.
- If you can't see if other traffic is approaching a hill or curve while you are approaching it. On one and two lane roads, this is quite dangerous.
- At driveways and junctions.
- Unless there is enough room to get back to your lane.

Navigating Obstacles: Strategies for Getting By Safely on the Road

When you intend to pass on a motorway:

- Check your blind spots by looking behind you.
- Take up a passing lane.
- Indicate your intention to pass.
- Increase your speed to pass the car.
- Return to your usual lane after giving a signal.

You may only pass to the right when: Understanding the Conditions for Safe Right-side Overtaking:

- The driver in front of you turns left, so you may pass on the right without risk. If the driver indicates a left turn, never pass on the left.
- A motorway has at least two lanes travelling in your direction.
- The street you're on is one-way.

Never use a portion of the road that is not paved or heavily trafficked to pass.

Safely Yielding: Understanding How to Respond When Being Passed on the Road

Let a vehicle to pass if it is passing you or signals that it will pass. Keep your pace and lane position constant.

Parking

- Mastering Parallel Parking: Techniques and Strategies for Confident Manoeuvres

- Parallel parking is when you park in a space parallel to the road and other parked vehicles. Parallel parking
- • Pull up alongside the vehicle in front of the parking space to approach it. Allow approximately two feet between your vehicle and the vehicle in front of you.
- • Get a place. Select a spot that is at least three feet longer than your vehicle. When you locate a parking space, activate your turn signal to signify your intent to park.
- • Search for vulnerable areas. Check your rearview mirror and the area behind you for approaching vehicles and pedestrians.
- • Stop when the front of your parking space and your rear fender are aligned. Maintain your signal.
- • Maintain an upright posture. Start turning the steering wheel away from the obstruction when your rear wheel is less than 18 inches from it. To realign, you must simultaneously draw forward and backward. Your vehicle should be parallel to the curb and 18 inches distant at this point.
- • Start reversing. To reverse into the parking space, turn the steering wheel 45 degrees.
- • After turning the vehicle off, engage the parking brake. Before exiting your vehicle, check carefully for oncoming automobiles, bicycles and motorcycles. When it is secure to do so, depart.

Straight-Line Stability

1. In a straight line, back up.
2. Signal. Turn signal on before approaching the curb. Once the turn signal is finished, turn it off.
3. Traffic inspection Watch the traffic and look in the proper blind spots.
4. Look for any blind spots. Check for approaching vehicles and pedestrians in your rearview mirror and behind you.
5. Start reversing now. Remaining within three feet of the curb, return in a straight line for three vehicle lengths. When backing up, pay attention to what is behind you.

6. Control. Back up at a steady, safe speed and adjust the steering wheel to keep the car under control. Practice until you can maintain a straight line in the car. To move away from the curb, repeat steps 1 and 2.

Hillside Parking for Safe and Secure Parking on Inclined Surfaces

If something goes wrong, your car might roll when you park it on a hill. Remember to engage the parking brake and leave the car in park or, if it has a manual transmission, in gear. To stall:

<u>Sloped Driveway Navigation:</u>

Set the parking brake, keep the car in drive, and turn the wheels so it won't roll into the street.

<u>Descending Safely:</u>

Steer your front wheels right towards the roadside or towards the curb.

<u>Going uphill:</u>

Allow your car to drift back a few inches while you turn your front wheels (to the left) away from the curb. The wheel ought to lightly contact the curb.

<u>When there is no curb, moving either upwards or downwards:</u>

If the brakes fail, turn the wheels so the car will drift away from the middle of the road.

Understanding Parking Regulations and Restrictions based on Curb Colors

Parking regulations are different along painted-color curbs.

- **Red:** No standing, parking, or stopping in a red zone.
- **Blue:** Special placard or license plate parking for a disabled person or a driver of a disabled person.
- **Green:** Park for a brief period. The time limit may be painted on the curb or displayed on signs.
- **White:** Halt for the duration necessary to pick up or drop off passengers.
- **Yellow:** Load and unload cargo as well as passengers. Never pause for more time than is indicated. You are typically expected to remain with your car if you operate a noncommercial vehicle.

Unlawful Parking Violations

Here are inappropriate locations to park your vehicle:

- Within 15 feet of a fire hydrant
- Between a curb and safety zone
- Double parking
- Within 3 feet of a wheelchair ramp
- Before or on a curb with a wheelchair ramp
- In a diagonal striped area near an accessible spot
- Where a "No Parking" sign is posted
- On a crosswalk (marked or unmarked)
- In front of a driveway or partially on a sidewalk
- In an electric vehicle charging spot unless you have an electric vehicle
- In a tunnel or on a bridge unless allowed
- On the wrong side of the road or highway except in:

An emergency

When directed by police

Where stopping is expressly permitted

If stopping on a highway:

- Park completely off the road
- Stay in your car with doors locked
- If parked for over 4 hours, your vehicle may be towed.

In summary, do not park:

- Near fire hydrants/fire stations
- In safety zones, wheelchair ramps
- Where "No Parking" signs are posted
- In lanes of travel

- Where it blocks driveways/sidewalks
- In EV charging spots without an EV

Only stop or park in designated areas to avoid towing, ticketing and ensuring safety.**Law Enforcement Stops: Understanding Your Rights and Responsibilities During Traffic Stops**

<u>During a Stop by Police Enforcement here's what to do:</u>

- To convey to the officer that you see him, turn on your right turn signal.
- Even if you're in the carpool/HOV lane, move entirely onto the right shoulder. When feasible, stop in a well-lit place.
- Switch off the radio.
- Until the officer tells you to exit your car, stay within it.
- After stopping, roll down your window before the police approach you.
- Before the officer contacts the driver or any other passenger, they should all hold their hands out in front of them.

Beginning on January 1, 2024, law enforcement officers must explain the cause for a traffic or pedestrian halt before conducting an interview regarding a criminal investigation or traffic violation. If the officer believes in good faith that concealing the reason is necessary to protect people or property from an imminent peril, an exception is made. G66-21B (CA) 32 The citation issued or completed police report must include the reason for the stop.

Chapter 3: Laws and Traffic Regulations

3.1 Traffic Management

Yield to pedestrians, bicycles, and other close vehicles that may have the right-of-way while at or approaching traffic signals or signs. See Who Goes First under the Right of Way Regulations section.

3.2 Traffic Signals

Solid Red Light

When the traffic light is red, you must STOP. At a red signal, you may turn right if:

- There isn't a posted NO Enter ON RED sign.
- When the situation is safe to turn, you halt at the halt or limit line and give way to pedestrians.

Red Arrow

Red arrows indicate STOP. A red arrow must not be followed. Hold your position until a green arrow or traffic signal appears.

Flashing Red Lights

A red signal light that is flashing signals STOP. When it is safe to move after halting, do so.

Solid Yellow Light

A yellow traffic signal light indicates CAUTION. Red is about to appear in the light. If you can safely stop when you observe a yellow traffic signal light, do so. Cross the junction with caution if you can't stop safely.

Yellow Arrow,

A yellow arrow denotes the conclusion of the protected turning period. The signal will shortly change. Complete your turn slowly if you can't safely stop or are already at the intersection. Watch out for the next signal. It might be a:

- A red or green traffic light.
- The color is red.

Flashing Yellow Lights

A flashing yellow traffic signal light signifies a cautionary signal to proceed slowly. Be mindful and move slowly. There's no need to halt.

Flashing Yellow Arrow

Although you can turn, it is not shielded from other traffic. After yielding to oncoming traffic, proceed cautiously and make a left turn.

A Constant Green Light

Green indicates you are going at a traffic light. Even so, you must stop if there is a car, a bicycle, or a pedestrian in the junction. Only move forward if there is sufficient room to avoid endangering approaching vehicles, cyclists, or pedestrians. Only go through the intersection if you can cross entirely before the traffic signal light goes red.

Green Arrow

A green arrow indicates that you should move in the direction it is pointing. With the green arrow, you can turn safely. Upon approaching traffic, a red traffic light stops the oncoming car.

Not Functioning Traffic Lights

When a traffic signal is broken, stop as if there are STOP signs in every direction controlling the intersection. When it is safe to do so, then move forward gently.

3.3 Pedestrian Signals or Signs

WALK or Person Walking

You are free to cross the road.

Do Not Raise Your Hands or Walk

It is forbidden to cross the street.

DON'T WALK flashing or flashing a raised hand.

Don't begin to cross the street. The light at the intersection is going to change. Even if they DON'T WALK signal is flashing, drivers must still yield to pedestrians.

Numbers

The numbers indicate the number of remaining seconds for street crossing.

Parallel Crossing

These crisscross and diagonal crosswalks let people cross the intersection simultaneously in all directions. Only cross the street when the WALK signal permits.

Sound

Beeping, chirping, or verbal cues can all be used to guide blind or visually impaired individuals across the street.

Push Button for Pedestrians

By doing so, the WALK or Walking Person signal is activated.

Lack of Pedestrian Signaling

Observe the traffic lights for vehicles if there are no pedestrian signals.

3.4 Signs

A road sign's shape can reveal just even more about its message as can its shade.

Octagon: Completely during traffic halts.

Horizontal Rectangle: Normally for directional signals

Pennant: No zones for passing. Are in advance notice.

Triangle: Only when yield signs are present.

Pennant: No zones for passing. Are in advance notice.

Diamond: Just to alert drivers to potential or present hazards on the road or nearby.

Vertical Rectangle: For regulatory signage, typically.

Pentagon: School crossing and advance signs.

Round: Early warning signs for railroads.

Cross buck: Crossing of Railroad

Octagon: Stop Every stop sign is octagonal (8-sided). You must halt your automobile in its tracks at the authorized stop line when there is a stop sign.

If there is no clearly marked stop line, halt before entering the crosswalk on the near side of the crossing. If there isn't a crosswalk, wait as near to the crossing road as you can before entering the junction so you can see approaching cars clearly.

Triangle: Yield Give vehicles that are the person who is in your way right-of-way by moving slowly. If it's safe to proceed, you can do so slowly and without pausing. When there are sides roads merge onto major roadways, yield signs are typically put up.

Pennant: Null passing the region ahead of you is a no passing zone. You'll find this sign on the left side of the road, when you're driving.

Diamond: Warning Confined Bridge. These indicators alert you to potential hazards or exceptional circumstances. The sign's Language or symbols will explain why you should exercise cautious.

Pentagon: School Symbol, It has five sides indicates that a school is nearby. Watch out for kids.

School Crossing: Slower down and look out for kids crossing the road as you get closer to this sign. If required, halt. Follow crosswalk police instructions.

Alert Signs

These indications warn you in advance of any potential dangers. Drive carefully.

When Wet, Slippery. When it's raining, go slowly. Avoid accelerating or braking abruptly. Make quick, abrupt rotates at a slow pace.

Separated Highway Up Ahead. There are 2 one-way sections of the highway up ahead. Continue to the right.

Ends of Divided Highway The split roadway that you are now travelling on ends 350 to 500 feet ahead. You will then be on a two-way roadway. Go to the right.

Small Clearance. You shouldn't enter if your automobile is higher than the limit height shown on the sign.

Pedestrian Overpass. Watch out for those crossing the street? If needed, go more slowly or stop.

Broad Bridge. The bridge is large enough to accommodate two lanes of traffic while having a rather low clearance.

DIP. There is a low area on the route. If the dip is covered with water, go carefully and be ready to halt.

Supple shoulders. The soil is soft at the side of the road. Stay on the pavement unless it's an emergency.

One-lane overpass. The bridge's low width makes it possible for just one vehicle to traverse it at time. Make sure there isn't any oncoming traffic on the bridge before you cross.

End of pavement. The hard-surfaced pavement up ahead is replaced with a low-type surface, or earth road.

Correct Curve. Speed down and keep your left free. The highway will take a right bend.

Two curves. Next, the path will make a right turn before making a left. Reduce your speed, don't pass, and keep to the right.

Winding Highway There will be numerous twists in the future. Drive softly and with caution.

Truck Overpass. Trucks may enter the road or may cross it, so keep an eye out for them.

Road Cross. A lane separates the main highway up ahead. Keep an eye out for more left- and right-bound traffic.

Side Street Another road goes in the direction indicated and leads to the highway. Watches out for vehicles headed in that direction?

Quick right turn. The roadway will bend sharply to the right. Reduce your speed, stay to the right, and steer clear of overtaking other vehicles.

A narrowing of lanes Up ahead, there won't be as many lanes. Traffic on the left must combine. Drivers in the left lane are necessary to let others to merge smoothly. The right lane's end.

Speed Warning Sign. 25 mph is the safest pace you should go at as you approach the next bend. With advisory speed signs, any warning sign in the form of a diamond is acceptable.

Hill/Downgrade. Reduce your speed and be ready to downshift to maintain braking control.

Yield Forward. Please obey the yield sign. Reduce your speed and prepare to either stop at a yield sign or change it to match the direction of traffic.

Traffic Light Up Front. Warning from the traffic light at the next junction. Slow down; there may be limited visibility.

Stop Sign in Front. As you get closer to this sign, slow down so you can be ready to stop at the stop sign check.

Ahead is two-way traffic. The one-way street or road is about to come to an end. You will then be facing flowing traffic at that moment.

3.5 Railroad crossing signals and signs

There are several signs, lights, and pavement markings that identify train crossings at highways. When you spot one of them, go more slowly and be ready to stop.

Trains are unable to halt suddenly. When travelling at 30 MPH, a normal freight train requires more than half a mile to halt. Longer trains travelling at faster speeds could need to halt for up to 1.5 kilometers.

When the mechanical or electrical alerting devices are displaying, the crossing gate is reduced, a human flagger is alerting of a nearing train, any pedestrian or person operating a vehicle nearing a railroad highway grade crossing should stop inside of 50 feet but just not less than 15 feet from the nearest rail of the railroad. Wait until you can advance safely before doing so.

Roadway marking

Pavement signs comprising of an RXR accompanied by a stop line nearer to the rails may be painted on the paved approaches to a crossing. Every pedestrian or motorist crossing the roadway should stop within 50 feet, but no nearer than 15 feet. Stay the behind stop line and watch for the train.

Warning Sign In Advance

The advance warning sign is often the first one you see as you approach a highway-rail junction. The advance warning sign instructs you to slow down, listen for trains, watch for them, and be prepared to stop if you see one.

Buck-cross sign

Junctions for the railroad and the roadway often include Crossbuck signage. There are yielding signs. The law requires you to yield to trains. You should slow down, listen for a train, and then stop when you see one coming. Where the road crosses the rails, a sign below the Crossbuck will indicate how many tracks are there.

Red Light Signs That Flash

Numerous highway-rail crossings have bells and flashing red lights installed by The Crossbuck. When the lights begin to flash, stop! A train is approaching. You cannot stop on the tracks or within six feet of either rail. Wait until you can go forward risk-free. If there are many tracks, be sure they are all clear of traffic before attempting to cross. Make sure there is room for your automobile on the opposite side before crossing in a congested location.

Gates

At crossings, bells and flashing red lights are often seen on gates. When the lights begin to flash and the gate begins to fall over your side of the roadway, halt. Wait until the gates are open and the lights stop flashing before proceeding since there could be a train approaching on a **neighboring** track.

While approaching railway and highway **crossings** proceed with caution and **are** prepared to stop if required. Pay special attention while driving following buses or trucks since they may have to stop at highway-railroad crossing even though the gates are closed and the warning lights are not blinking.

If your car stops on the rails, don't hesitate. As soon as you can, get out of the car with your passengers. The safest route is towards the train, but if a collision is likely to happen, it stays off the tracks. By doing this, the possibility that you'll be hurt by your automobile or any collision-related debris is decreased.

3.6 Construction and Maintenance Traffic Control Signs

In road building and maintenance work zones, several traffic control systems are used to safeguard the safety of highway workers as well as motorists and pedestrians. Be prepared to slow down and use care when a sign, flagger, or police officer requests it. Construction and maintenance signs alert drivers to unusual or possibly dangerous conditions in or around work zones. In areas where roads and streets are being built, diamond-shaped signage is widely utilized.

Channeling Apparatus

The most common obstacles used to alert drivers to unusual or potentially dangerous conditions in highway and street repair zones include barriers, vertical panels, drums, and cones. These gadgets, which may include caution lights for use at night, are intended to safely guide traffic through the work zone. Never go along a route that has a closed sign. Look for a detour or an alternative route. The stripes on barricades and panel barriers slope downwards in the direction that cars must go.

3.7 Guidelines for Right-of-Way: Who Moves First?

Right-of-way laws determine who moves first when cars, bikes, and pedestrians encounter. First-coming cars have right-of-way. The right-of-way driver must yield to pedestrians, cyclists, and autos. Never assume other drivers will yield. Provide means to avoid crashes.

3.8 Intersections

Intersections are where roadways meet. Traffic signals are illuminated at controlled junctions. Unmanaged and inaccessible intersections do not. Be sure to look for cars, bicycles, and pedestrians before crossing an intersection. Be ready to reduce your speed and even halt if required. The right-of-way is always given to pedestrians. Following are some guidelines for intersection right-of-way:

- When there is no STOP or YIELD signs, the first car to reach the intersection has the right-of-way. Give the right-of-way to the car, person on foot, or person riding a bicycle on your right if they arrive at the intersection concurrently with you. When approaching a stop sign with a stop sign on each of its four corners, stop first and continue as usual.
- At T crossroads without a STOP or YIELD sign, vehicles, cyclists, and pedestrians on the through route have the right-of-way to proceed.
- When turning left, be aware of pedestrians.
- When making a right turn, always look out for pedestrians crossing the street and vehicles riding next to you on motorbikes and bicycles.

- When it is Green traffic signal light, drive carefully. They have the right-of-way, for pedestrians.
- Moving cautiously and giving way to any existing traffic using the lanes. When there is not enough room to fully cross the crossing before the traffic signal light turns red, stopping or blocking the intersection is illegal.

3.9 Roundabouts

In a roundabout, traffic circles a central island in one direction.

Using a roundabout:

- Go more slowly as you get closer.
- Give way to all oncoming cars on the roundabout.
- When there is sufficient space in the traffic flow to merge safely, turn right.
- Watch for lane markers and signage that direct you.
- Circumambulate in a clockwise motion. Do not pass or stop.
- Use a signal to depart or change lanes.
- If you fail to find your exit, turn around and head back.
- Choose the entry or exit lane depending on your destination if the roundabout has multiple lanes.

3.10 Pedestrians

These individuals are regarded as vulnerable road users or pedestrians:

- A person on foot.
- A person who commutes by means other than a car or bicycle. This includes skateboards, roller skates, etc.
- A handicapped person who travels by tricycle, quadricycle, or wheelchair.

Although having the right-of-way, pedestrians are nevertheless required to abide by the laws of the road. You must proceed cautiously, slow down, or stop when a pedestrian is crossing a road, whether or not there is a crosswalk, to ensure they can do so safely.

3.11 Crosswalks

A pedestrian crosswalk is a section of the road specifically designed for pedestrians to safely cross the street. They frequently have white lines as a delineating feature.

Yellow crosswalk stripes are sometimes painted at intersections near schools. There are certain crosswalks that do not have markings. Pedestrians always have the right of way in crosswalks, whether marked or unmarked. If there is a limit line before the crosswalk, drivers are expected to come to a complete stop at the limit line and give pedestrians the right of way. In certain crosswalks, flashing lights are installed. Always watch for pedestrians and be prepared to stop regardless of whether or not the lights in the intersection are blinking.

3.12 Braking

At the same speed, stopping a large vehicle or a commercial truck takes longer than stopping a passenger car. As they move, they leave extra room in front of their car for when they might need to stop quickly. At 55 mph, the typical passenger car can come to a complete stop in less than 300 feet. Large vehicles can take up to 400 feet to halt when moving at the same pace. A loaded truck will require more time to stop than an empty truck since stopping safely takes longer the heavier and faster the vehicle is travelling. Avoid moving before a big vehicle and stopping or slowing down abruptly. The big car won't be able to stop quickly enough to avoid hitting you.

3.13 Missing Spots (the No Zone)

Drivers of large vehicles and trucks benefit from larger mirrors and a better view in front of them. Yet, they also have many blind zones, sometimes called No Zones. A truck or large vehicle driver may not see your car in these places. The truck driver won't be able to see you if you can't be seen in the truck's side mirrors.

3.14 Turning

The rear wheels of a car turn on a shorter path than the front wheels. The difference in the length of the turning path increases with vehicle length. This is why drivers of heavy cars and trucks frequently have to swing wide to make a turn. Look at the turn signals of the large car you are following before you begin to pass. Although it may be turning in one direction, it is turning by swinging widely in the opposite direction.

3.15 Maneuvering

Trucks and large vehicles are more difficult to maneuver than passenger cars. They may be driven in the lane directly to the left of the far-right lane on a divided highway with four or more traffic lanes travelling in one direction. Avoid the following when driving near big trucks and vehicles:

- Alternate lanes in front of them to get to a turn or an exit.
- Continue to drive next to them longer than necessary. Always pass over a big car on the left. Move before the big car or truck once you've passed it. It is challenging for the driver to avoid road hazards when a large vehicle is nearby.
- Neglect to consider their size and speed.

3.16 Work Zones and Road Workers

You will notice warning signs and message boards when there are workers, sluggish equipment, or blocked roads up ahead.

Carefully navigate the work area by:

- Deceleration.
- Leaving more room between cars.
- Anticipating an abrupt slowdown or stop.
- Maintaining vigilance for lane-changers.
- Ignoring diversion.

Cones, drums, or other barriers will direct you through the work zone. Be prepared to stop or slow down for any highway machinery. When it is safe, merge without going over the drums or cones. If lanes are congested, or the shoulder is blocked, be alert for bicycles. Follow any instructions from staff members, such as flaggers or special signs.

3.17 Vehicles Carrying Dangerous Loads

If a truck has a diamond-shaped sign, it implies that its load can be hazardous (gas, explosives etc.). These signs require drivers to stop before crossing railroad tracks.

Chapter 4: California DMV Permit Practice Test 1 (50)

1. Start in the right lane and end in: To turn right onto such a two-way road from the two-way street, begin in the right lane and end in:

    a) Every lane that is open.

    b) Lane to the left.

    c) The lane that is nearest the curb.

2. Pedestrians have the right-of-way when crossing at corners:

    a) Only when the street has been painted with a crosswalk.

    b) If a crosswalk has been marked or not.

    c) Just at unobstructed junctions.

3. The following are all hazardous when driving. Which is also prohibited?

    a) Turning on a light or lights inside.

    b) Wearing an ear-covering headset on both ears

    c) in residential streets, using cruise control.

4. Who needs to use seatbelts?

    a) All passengers who are under the age of 21 and the driver.

    b) The driver and every passenger who is at least 8 years old or who is 4 feet 9 inches or taller.

    c) The driver and those in the front seats.

5. When you notice a NEV ROUTE sign, be cautious of the following:

    a) A law enforcement official in Nevada.

    b) Automobiles on the road driving slowly.

    c) Vehicles drawn by animals.

6. You want to cross a junction directly and the traffic light is green. In the event that a car has already entered the crossing and is turning, you must:

    a) Then stop as you enter the junction.

    b) Cross the junction in your car. The right-of-way is yours.

    c) Before you approach the intersection, allow that car to finish its turn.

7. At the next intersection, you want to turn right. Slow down and perform the following:

    a) Stay out of the bicycle lane when driving.

    b) The left side of your lane as you travel forward.

    c) Provide a 100-foot warning before turning.

8. The day is really windy. When you're driving, a dust storm crosses the motorway, making it harder to see. You should slow down and activate your:

    a) Internal lighting

    b) Headlights.

    c) Parking lamps

9. If there are no "Stop" or "Yield" signs at a junction, you must:

    a) Whenever car or bicycle arrives first, please yield.

    b) Consider the intersection to be a roundabout.

    c) If a vehicle approaches the crossing at the same moment as you, yield to the car on your left.

10. Which of the following claims regarding drugs and traffic is accurate?

    a) Even over-the-counter medications can make you unable to drive.

    b) If you don't feel sleepy, using any prescription medication is safe.

    c) Only unlawful drugs can make you unable to drive.

11. What should you do first while making a three-point turn?

    a) After giving a left turn signal, carefully scan the area for oncoming traffic.

    b) After making a left turn, cross the street and halt facing the edge of the pavement.

    c) Turn your right turn signal on, then stop and pull over to the right.

12. What do signs in the shape of pennants mean?

    a) A crossing for schools

    b) Unsafe Passing Zone

    c) Yield

13. In the up-coming intersection, you must halt. There are railroad tracks you must cross just before the crossroads. When: You should pull over before crossing the train tracks.

   a) **There isn't enough room for you to fully cross the tracks.**
   b) The crossing is situated in a city or town where trains run often.
   c) You drive a passenger car with two or more kids.

14. On your side of the street, a school bus has halted and is now blinking its red lights. What ought you to do?

   a) Wait until every youngster has crossed the street before stopping.
   b) **As soon as the red lights are flashing, stop.**
   c) When you feel it is safe to continue, stop first.

15. What side effects are expected if you combine alcohol with another drug?

   a) There are none unless the medication is prescribed-only.
   b) There are no side effects when using over-the-counter medication.
   c) **Both the booze and the medicine have stronger effects.**

16. Drivers should: when parked on a public highway

   a) **Go as far away from the road as you can.**
   b) Never park on the right side of the street.
   c) The aforementioned.

17. Blind areas around a big vehicle are larger than those around a small vehicle.

   a) **Deeper and bigger**
   b) Shorter and narrower
   c) Less hazardous

18. The following rules apply to the posted speed in a business district:

   a) **25 mph**
   b) 30 mph
   c) 35 mph

19. When there are no "Stop" or "Yield" signs at a crossroads, you must:

   a) Observe the intersection's traffic and pedestrians' rights.

b) If a vehicle approaching the junction from your right arrives at the same moment as you, stop.

c) The aforementioned.

20. The intersection is blocked by cars as you approach a green signal. What action should you take?

    a) Make a partial entrance to the intersection to claim the right-of-way.

    b) Once you enter the intersection, hold off until all traffic has stopped.

    c) Wait until you can cross entirely before proceeding through the junction.

21. You are following a big truck on the motorway. You ought to drive:

    a) Compared to a passenger car, the truck is further behind.

    b) Wait to pass on the truck's right side.

    c) More closely than for a passenger car behind the truck.

22. What else should motorists do in the event that their brakes fail?

    a) Attach a white cloth to the handle of the left door.

    b) Brake minimally.

    c) Make a lower gear change.

23. Parking is prohibited

    a) The tunnel.

    b) On the side of a car parked facing the road.

    c) The aforementioned.

24. The space _____ of your vehicle is subject to the "three-second rule."

    a) On either side

    b) Ahead

    c) In the rear

25. How may weariness be avoided on a lengthy journey?

    a) Obtain adequate rest.

    b) Arrange to travel great distances by car with a friend.

    c) The aforementioned.

26. Which one of the following raises your risk of colliding with something?

a) Shifting lanes to pass other vehicles continuously.

b) Before you begin driving, make sure your rearview mirror is adjusted.

c) Keeping an eye on your back while changing lanes.

27. What should you do as soon as your wheels veer off the pavement?

   a) **Lift your foot off the gas and softly use the brakes.**

   b) To alert other drivers, pull over to the right and honk your horn.

   c) Reverse the direction of the wheel.

28. If you're driving on ice or snow that is slick:

   a) To prevent your brakes from freezing, pump them.

   b) **A low gear should be selected before descending steep hills.**

   c) Keep traction by closely following other vehicles.

29. If a lap belt and a separate shoulders belt are present in a vehicle, you are:

   a) **Necessary to wear both the shoulder and lap belt.**

   b) Only necessary while wearing a shoulder belt.

   c) Only necessary to wear a lap belt.

30. You are in front of a green light, but the traffic on the opposite side of the intersection prevents you from passing through the entire intersection. How do you proceed?

   a) See the subsequent green light.

   b) **To avoid blocking the intersection, wait until the traffic in front has cleared.**

   c) After waiting for the traffic to clear, enter the intersection.

31. A yellow light that flashes:

   a) Warns drivers to drive carefully.

   b) Is applied at intersections that are risky.

   c) **The aforementioned.**

32. When a traffic light has a red arrow pointing to the right, you may:

   a) As soon as you come to a complete halt, turn in that direction.

   b) Slow down, look for traffic, and then turn that way.

   c) **Wait till the light turns green before making that turn.**

33. It is legal to drive when you're under the influence of any medicine that inhibits your ability to drive:

   a) Not at all.
   b) If a doctor had prescribed the drug.
   c) Whether your vehicle is consistently insured.

34. Every driver who is 21 years of age or older and has a blood alcohol content (BAC) of _____ or above is prohibited from operating a vehicle.

   a) 0.05%
   b) 0.10%
   c) 0.08%

35. Which statement regarding safety belts is accurate?

   a) These can lessen accidents and fatalities.
   b) They might keep you confined to a car.
   c) When travelling within the city, they are not required.

36. Which action should be avoided when driving close to pedestrians?

   a) On a sidewalk, drive.
   b) Pass a car that is at a crosswalk and halted.
   c) The aforementioned.

37. Your BAC is based on the following:

   a) How long it takes between sips?
   b) Your alcohol consumption.
   c) Those above.

38. Drivers should look further ahead on a motorway than they would on a city street normally:

   a) Due to the fact that stopping a car on a motorway requires 500 feet.
   b) To recognize potential risks and dangers up ahead.
   c) Thus there are numerous lanes.

39. When your car is submerged in water, you should:

   a) Wait for the water to flood in before exhaling slowly through your nose.
   b) Make an instant call to the fire department.

c) Before it begins to sink, get out.

40. Who is most in danger?

   a) Motorists who are worn out.

   b) Motorists who are on lengthy, monotonous routes.

   c) The aforementioned.

41. A driver threatens a pedestrian or another driver or cuts off another vehicle. Here are several instances of

   a) Excessive speed

   b) Driving defensively

   c) Traffic rage

42. On any motorway, use the far left (last) lane when moving slowly in front of traffic.

   a) It cannot lead to a traffic ticket.

   b) This causes other drivers to slow down, therefore saving lives.

   c) It can aggravate and irritate other motorists.

43. You are nearing a crossroads. The red flashing traffic light is present. What ought you to do?

   a) Drive cautiously through the intersection to the other side.

   b) Before entering, pause. Before moving forward, watch for the green signal.

   c) When it is safe to continue, stop before entering.

44. Tailgating:

   a) The practice of defensive driving.

   b) It cannot lead to a traffic ticket.

   c) It can aggravate and irritate other motorists.

45. There is no crosswalk or stop line at a stop sign. You need to halt:

   a) Prior to approaching the intersection.

   b) If you can clearly see the traffic on the intersecting road after you enter the intersection.

   c) At the next intersection.

46. A bicycle is riding on the right edge of your lane, and you want to pass them. You:

    a) Can't squeeze past the biker on a bicycle.

    b) May not, for whatever reason, pass the bicyclist.

    c) Before passing the bicycle, you must sound your horn.

47. Parking is not allowed:

    a) In a space with a crosshatched (diagonal) pattern.

    b) Unless otherwise noted, in a bike lane.

    c) A 20-foot distance from a railroad track.

48. Your car cannot be parked:

    a) In an emergency, on the side of the highway.

    b) 100 feet or less from an elementary school.

    c) Next to a curb with red paint.

49. The letters ABS stand for:

    a) Asphalt-Braking System.

    b) Anti-Braking System.

    c) Anti-lock Brake System.

50. It would help if you didn't go around another car:

    a) On a one-way roadway with many lanes.

    b) Where traffic is most likely to enter or cross.

    c) When the left side of your lane has a broken yellow line.

Chapter 5: California DMV Permit Practice Test 2 (50)

1. A railroad advanced notice sign has what shape?

    a) Crossbuck

    b) Pentagon

    c) Round

2. What makes nighttime driving more challenging than daytime driving?

    a) The legislation requires that headlights be used.

    b) Maintaining a safe distance.

    c) Diminished visibility

3. You notice a car coming up from behind. You no longer see the car when you recheck your mirror to change lanes. You ought to:

    a) Turn on your signal, and then do a gentle lane change.

    b) To make sure the car isn't in your blind zone, look behind you.

    c) To determine whether the car is in your blind spot, look in your outside mirror.

4. At a junction, there is a minor crash that you are a part of. No one is hurt, and the cars only sustain minor damage. You ought to:

    a) As soon as law enforcement is on the way, leave your car in the right-hand lane.

    b) If it's possible, move your car out of the traffic lane.

    c) Please don't relocate your car for any reason.

5. When leaving a car park, you should:

    a) Must only make a left or right turn if it's safe to do so.

    b) Possess the right of way.

    c) Must stop before the oncoming traffic and yield.

6. When the intersection is blocked by traffic but you have a green light, you should:

    a) Once entering the intersection, wait for the traffic to clear.

    b) Try to avoid the traffic by merging into another lane.

    c) As soon as the traffic has cleared, avoid the intersection.

7. While leaving your car parked on a hill:

a) If there is no curb, your front wheels should be level to the road.

b) Use the parking brake and put the car in "park" or drive away.

c) You should have one of your rear wheels contact the curb.

8. Regulatory signs are:

   a) Warnings

   b) Law

   c) Suggestions

9. Your BAC is based on:

   a) How much alcohol you consume.

   b) The kind of drink you consume.

   c) Your level of fitness

10. In commercial areas, U-turns are:

    a) Whenever approaching cars do not pose a risk.

    b) Only permitted at junctions unless specifically forbidden by a sign.

    c) Always forbidden.

11. What are you supposed to do as you get ready to make a right turn at a crosswalk?

    a) Do not turn in front of a biker without first giving them a turn signal and checking for them.

    b) Bicyclists travelling in the other direction must yield.

    c) Make a horn noise.

12. Unless otherwise indicated, what is the top speed limit for two-lane, undivided highways?

    a) 55 mph

    b) 65 mph

    c) 45 mph

13. If you park close to a curb, switch your turn signals on:

    a) When approaching or leaving the curb.

    b) When approaching the curb without moving away from it.

    c) Only after stepping off the curb.

14. When the going is slick, you ought to

- a) Put the brakes on.
- b) Abruptly and carefully brake.
- **c) Use the brakes gradually and steadily.**

15. A car coming out of a driveway and into a road:

    - a) Possesses the right of way.
    - **b) Must come to a complete stop and give pedestrians and other road users the right-of-way.**
    - c) It has the right-of-way over cars from the left but must yield to traffic from the right.

16. Which children need child restraint equipment?

    - a) The height of a six-year-old is 4 feet 10 inches.
    - **b) The height of a seven-year-old is 4 feet 7 inches.**
    - c) The height of an eight-year-old is 4 feet 9 inches.

17. BAC is:

    - a) Beer Accumulation abbreviated.
    - b) How much alcohol is in your blood in ounces?
    - **c) How much alcohol is in your blood?**

18. A left turn is desired at the crossroads up ahead. From the opposite direction, a car approaches the intersection and drives straight forward. You:

    - **a) Before making a turn, you must wait for the car to pass through.**
    - b) If the signal is green, you may not approach the junction to be ready for your left turn.
    - c) Can make a left turn. I must give way to you.

19. When your accelerator sticks, you should:

    - a) Shutting off the ignition while the car is in motion.
    - b) Avoid using the brakes. Lift your foot off the gas and adjust the front wheels.
    - **c) Put the gearshift in neutral, hit the brakes, and attempt to safely move the vehicle off the road.**

20. Drivers must keep take mind that motorbikes can _____ than other cars when following one.

a) Accelerated significantly

b) Stopping significantly faster

c) Stop more gradually

21. A speeding ticket may be issued if the driver exceeds the posted speed limit:

    a) Under no circumstances.

    b) If you are transporting multiple passengers.

    c) If road conditions or weather dictate a slower speed.

22. You wish to park uphill on a two-way street with no curb. Which direction do the front wheels turn?

    a) Hence, they face forward.

    b) Turn left, towards the road's centre.

    c) To the right, along the side of the road.

23. You must make a right turn at the intersection upon approaching a roundabout with several lanes. You must:

    a) Choose either lane or exit the lane from which you entered.

    b) Use the rightmost lane and the rightmost exit lane.

    c) Select the left lane and exit

24. If any of the following apply, Within 10 days of a California traffic accident, you must provide a Report of Road Occurrence Of a hazardous event in California (SR 1).

    a) Refinancing the outstanding sum of your auto loan.

    b) Are involved in an accident that costs $1,000 in damages.

    c) Plan to be away of the country for over 45 days.

25. Which of these roadways freezes first following precipitation?

    a) Tunnels

    b) Intersections

    c) Bridges and flyovers

26. While preparing to turn left from a one-way road into another one-way road:

    a) Move to the left lane or the left side of a single-lane roadway.

    b) Move to the right lane or the right shoulder of a single-lane roadway.

    c) Move to the right lane or the left side of a single-lane roadway.

27. Which direction should the front wheels face when parked on an incline next to a curb?

   a) To the curbside.

   b) Perpendicular to the curb.

   c) Nowhere near the curb.

28. You may use the shoulder to pass other vehicle:

   a) If the car in front of you is turning left.

   b) If there are two or more lanes in your direction of travel.

   c) Under no circumstances.

29. You must proceed straight through an intersection as you approach a roundabout with several lanes. You must:

   a) Choose either lane and exit the lane from which you entered.

   b) Use the rightmost lane and the rightmost exit lane.

   c) Select the left lane and exit.

30. Use the following when driving in foggy, snow, or rain:

   a) Running lights.

   b) High-beam headlights.

   c) There are low-beam headlights.

31. A traffic sign containing a red circle and a slash above a symbol indicates:

   a) The maneuver represented by the symbol is prohibited.

   b) The maneuver indicated by the warning must be carried out with extreme caution.

   c) Do not exceed the speed restriction set on the road.

32. To safely reverse a vehicle, motorists should NOT:

   a) They honk their horn before to backing up.

   b) Check your vehicle before to entering.

   c) Examine their shoulder as they retreat.

33. If an oncoming car in front of you has begun to turn left:

   a) Maintain your current speed and yield the right of way.

   b) Beep your horn to alert the driver and keep your speed constant.

c) Stop or slow down to avoid a collision.

34. What occurs if two vehicles arrive simultaneously at a four-way stop sign intersection?

   a) The right-hand driver concedes to the left-hand driver.

   b) The left-hand driver yields to the right-hand driver.

   c) The first car to arrive must yield at the intersection.

35. Typically, the first sign vehicles see as they approach a highway-rail crossing is:

   a) The crossbuck symbol.

   b) There is a speed restriction sign.

   c) An early warning signal.

36. When approaching a junction, a motorist:

   a) Gets priority over traffic already present in the intersection.

   b) You must proceed through the crossing, even if another car is there.

   c) Must yield to traffic already present in the intersection.

37. You must use turn signals to convey your purpose with sufficient time for other cars to perceive them:

   a) BEFORE you relocate.

   b) AFTER you relocate.

   c) if it's raining outside.

38. Which statement concerning bikers and automobile drivers is true?

   a) Motorcycles are heavier than other vehicles and are therefore less affected by wind and precipitation.

   b) During busy road circumstances, motorcyclists are not permitted to exceed the speed limit.

   c) Motorcycle riders have the same rights and duties as other drivers.

39. The maximum speed restriction in alleys is:

   a) 15 mph

   b) 20 mph

   c) 25 mph

40. You are required to yield to pedestrians with canes or guiding dogs:

a) **All the time.**

b) Only when the person is being led across the street by a guiding dog.

c) Only when there is a crossing guard present.

41. You should glance 10 to 15 sec ahead while driving.

    a) Because it's a legal necessity.

    b) And concentrate on the middle ground

    c) **Help identify potential dangers early.**

42. While following huge trucks, you should leave a greater distance between your car and the vehicle in front of you because:

    a) If you follow the vehicle too closely, you will be caught in its wind draught.

    b) **The additional room provides visibility surrounding the truck.**

    c) Their greater mass helps them to halt faster than you.

43. After entering the roundabout, cars proceed:

    a) **In the anticlockwise direction**

    b) In a clockwise manner.

    c) In either direction

44. When traveling at night with no oncoming traffic, a driver should:

    a) **High beams of light**

    b) Low-beam headlamps.

    c) Parking lights.

45. The state of California has a Fundamental Speed Law, which means:

    a) **Drivers may never exceed the acceptable speed limit for present conditions.**

    b) When it is rainy, foggy, windy, snowing, or dusty, drivers may disregard the imposed speed limit.

    c) Always drive ten miles per hour slower than the posted speed limit.

46. When a hazard is spotted in the distance, reaction distance:

    a) **It is the distance a vehicle may travel in ideal conditions before the driver applies the brakes.**

    b) Equals total stopping distance subtracted from perception distance.

c) It is the sum of the perceptual and stopping distances.

47. When may you only use your parking lights to drive?

    a) On days with poor visibility due to fog.

    b) 30 minutes after sunset or 30 minutes before sunrise.

    c) Under no circumstances.

48. It is prohibited to leave a youngster younger than ___ years old alone in a motor vehicle.

    a) 6

    b) 8

    c) 4

49. When parking _____ turn the front wheels towards the curb.

    a) Facing downhill,

    b) Facing uphill

    c) On a flat road.

50. When can driving with only parking lights be permitted?

    a) 30 minutes after sunset or 30 minutes before sunrise.

    b) On days with poor visibility due to fog.

    c) Under no circumstances.

Chapter 6: California DMV Permit Practice Test 3 (50)

1. Drivers are advised to inspect their rearview mirrors:

    a) Frequently observe the flow of traffic behind them.
    b) Just when decelerating.
    c) To determine whether a truck is in its blind spot.

2. Which of the following statements regarding the Anti-Lock Brake System is true?

    a) It permits steering during emergency braking situations.
    b) It inhibits sliding.
    c) All of the preceding.

3. At a crosswalk, a vehicle stops to allow a person to cross the roadway. The operator of a vehicle approaching from behind must:

    a) Pass and overtake the halted vehicle.
    b) Blare the horn.
    c) Not pass and overtake the halted car.

4. If a driver appears to be pulling out in front of you, the safest course of action is:

    a) Maintain your speed and sound your horn.
    b) Reduce your speed or come to a stop, and use your horn.
    c) Use your horn and enter the adjacent lane.

5. When is it permissible to leave a child under six years old unsupervised in a motor vehicle?

    a) If the youngster is accompanied by an adult of at least 12 years of age.
    b) When weather circumstances pose a risk to the child's health or safety.
    c) When keys are left in the ignition, harm may occur.

6. If any of the following apply to you, you need to report a traffic accident in California by filling out Form SR-1 with the DMV:

    a) You are part of a crash in which someone gets injured.
    b) Your vehicle failed a smog test.
    c) You switch insurance companies.

7. Which of these trucks must always stop at railroad crossings?

a) Tanker trucks are marked with placards for hazardous materials.

b) A boat trailer pulled by motorhomes or pickup pickups.

c) Any vehicle with three or more axles or over 4,000 pounds.

8. You are required to tell the DMV within 5 days if:

   a) Paint your vehicle a new colour.

   b) Transfer or sell your automobile.

   c) Receive a traffic violation citation.

9. Often, _____ are white rectangles with black lettering or symbols.

   a) Warning symptoms

   b) Destination signage (guide signs)

   c) Regulation markings

10. When the following conditions are met, it is safe to return to your lane after overtaking another vehicle:

    a) The driver you just overtook slows down so you may return to your lane.

    b) In your rearview mirror, you can see both headlights of the automobile you just passed.

    c) At least 50 feet separates you from the car you just passed.

11. In an uncontrolled intersection when you cannot see oncoming traffic until immediately before entering, the speed limit is:

    a) 15 mph

    b) 20 mph

    c) 25 mph

12. Legally, the operator of an emergency vehicle equipped with lights and a siren may:

    a) Speed above the speed limit

    b) Ignore red lights.

    c) All of the preceding.

13. Octagonal signs instruct drivers to:

    a) Be mindful of potential hazards ahead.

    b) Respect the speed restriction specified.

c) Stop completely at the designated stop line.

14. You must stop completely at a yield sign:

    a) Always.

    b) Whenever traffic conditions demand it.

    c) Never.

15. Several automobiles are approaching a four-way stop sign. Which party has the right of way?

    a) The driver who arrived at the crossroads last.

    b) The first driver to stop at the intersection.

    c) The driver on the left side of the vehicle.

16. If guilty of driving under the influence, you could be sentenced to the following:

    a) No jail time, but a $500 fine is required.

    b) Up to six months of prison time

    c) Serve up to one year in prison.

17. You wish to reverse out of a parking spot. Always move back carefully and observe:

    a) At your rear views when reversing.

    b) As you back up, you should look over your right and left shoulders.

    c) Use your side mirrors as you reverse.

18. If you are under 21 and your BAC on the breath test (PAS) is 0.01% or greater, you may be suspended for:

    a) 180 days

    b) 1 year

    c) 18 months

19. Are motorists permitted to exceed the speed limit when passing another vehicle?

    a) But, they must drive with prudence.

    b) No.

    c) Absolutely, but by no more than 10 mph.

20. If vehicles approaching a crossroads from opposite directions arrive at the same time:

a) A left-turning vehicle must yield to straight-moving and right-turning vehicles.

b) Straight-moving vehicles must yield to left-turning vehicles.

c) Right-turning vehicles must yield to straight-moving and left-turning vehicles.

21. If your vehicle begins to slide on a wet road and you should:

    a) Reduce your speed by changing to a lower gear.

    b) Gradually remove your foot from the gas pedal.

    c) Slow down by rapidly and firmly using the brakes.

22. You intend to consume a couple beers at the social event you attend with a group of pals. You need to:

    a) Make arrangements to ride home with a sober companion.

    b) Avoid switching between alcoholic beverages and nonalcoholic beverages.

    c) Make booze the focal point of the occasion.

23. Three of the most crucial moments to watch for traffic behind you are:

    a) Reversing, changing lanes, or decelerating hastily.

    b) Crossing crossings or trailing behind other vehicles.

    c) While reversing, making a quick turn, or crossing an intersection, use caution.

24. While one pedestrian is crossing your traffic lane, your red traffic light changes to green. The right of way must be granted:

    a) Pertaining to the pedestrian

    b) Via the pedestrian.

    c) By the pedestrian, but only when left-turning vehicles are present.

25. To be able to see automobiles in your blind areas, you must:

    a) Across your shoulders

    b) In the interior rearview mirror

    c) On the exterior rearview mirror

26. A police officer is signaling you to go to the roadway's edge. You choose to disregard the officer's caution and depart the scene. You have committed a misdemeanor and may be penalized by:

    a) Fines as high as $2,000

b) Issued an advisory and a citation.

c) Country jail sentence of no and over one year.

27. A white broken line:

    a) Indicates that overtaking or crossing is forbidden in that lane.

    b) Identifies the right side of the road.

    c) Provides separation between two lanes driving in the same way.

28. It is illegal for a person on probation for Driving Under the Influence (DUI) to operate a motor vehicle with a blood alcohol content (BAC) of _____ or higher.

    a) 0.08%, if the individual is at least 21 years old.

    b) 0.1%

    c) 0.01%

29. Which of the following is likewise unlawful, despite the fact that all of the others are risky to perform while driving?

    a) Dual headphones are being utilized to listen to music.

    b) The act of reading a road map.

    c) Altering your outside mirrors.

30. Continuous signaling is required while turning because:

    a) It is prohibited to switch off your indicator before a turn has been completed.

    b) Before completing a turn, it is never secure to switch off a signal.

    c) Notifies other drivers of your intentions.

31. Which of the below will prevent you from being rear-ended?

    a) Decreasing your following distance.

    b) Changing lanes frequently.

    c) Merge into another lane.

32. Which of these cars needs to come to a halt prior crossing railroad tracks?

    a) Placards for hazardous materials are shown on tank trucks.

    b) Pickup vehicles or motorhomes carrying a trailer

    c) Sport utility vehicles that can accommodate four or more people.

33. In the outer right lane of a motorway, you should:

    a) Must grant merging traffic the right-of-way.

b) **Should prepare for merging traffic at on-ramps.**

c) Obviously moving more slowly than other drivers.

34. On the opposite side of a split highway is a school bus having flashing red lights. You:

   a) Must reduce speed and get ready to halt.

   b) **Do not have to halt.**

   c) Must come to a complete stop and hold it until the flashing stops.

35. Whenever a yellow arrow shows for your lane, you are going to turn left from a designated left-turn lane. You ought to:

   a) **Be ready to follow the next signal that flashes by.**

   b) Under no circumstances should you turn or stop.

   c) To cross the junction, accelerate.

36. At the same time, two vehicles arrive at an uncontrolled crossroads. Who has the upper hand?

   a) **The right-hand driver.**

   b) The left-hand driver.

   c) No one.

37. Any railroad rails must not be crossed without first:

   a) Verify if there is space for your car on the opposite side.

   b) Observe and hear for trains.

   c) **The aforementioned.**

38. Drivers must abide by directions from:

   a) Other motorists whose cars are stuck on the road.

   b) Parking lots are patrolled by security personnel.

   c) **Construction sites have signal persons known as flaggers.**

39. Which of the below traffic lights requires you to stop your car at all times?

   a) There are red and yellow lights, as well as a steady red light.

   b) **Unlit road signs, pulsating red lights, and a steady red light.**

   c) Flashing yellow lights, red arrows, and solid red lights.

   d)

40. When driving beside a light rail car, you must:

   a) At an uncontrolled crossroads, may make a turn in front of an approaching light rail car.

   b) It is forbidden to use the lane next to a light rail vehicle.

   c) Should pay particular attention to all traffic lights because light rail vehicles have the potential to interfere with them.

41. When a passenger under the age of 18 is present, smoking inside a car is:

   a) The choice is up to the driver.

   b) If it's your child, it's legal.

   c) Unlawful.

42. If there's a solid yellow line next to a split yellow line, then:

   a) You may cross across the solid line.

   b) In both directions may pass.

   c) You may cross over the broken line.

43. While you're following a: Give yourself more room in front of your car.

   a) Passenger vehicle.

   b) Station wagon.

   c) Motorcycle.

44. Which of the given comments about turning signals is accurate?

   a) You must be given room by other vehicles if you signal for a lane change.

   b) Lane changes need signaling at all times.

   c) Never combine hand signals with electronic signals.

45. Which of the following statements regarding cars with diamond-shaped signs indicating hazardous loads is accurate?

   a) They can't go faster than 35 MPH.

   b) They cannot operate a vehicle on interstates.

   c) Before crossing railroad tracks, they must stop.

46. In the event of a collision, you must legally provide the following information about your driver's license with:

   a) Security personnel.

b) The other participants in the collision.

   c) Witnesses.

47. _____ your mirrors once you get ready to change lanes.

   a) Never rely upon

   b) Avoid using

   c) Always trust

48. You have been given the all-clear by a police officer to go after a red light. What ought you to do?

   a) Stop completely, then follow the officer's instructions.

   b) Follow the officer's instructions.

   c) The green light, please.

49. What of the following commands are most important to follow?

   a) Officer of the law

   b) Red light

   c) Stopped sign

50. A stop sign is what shape?

   a) Upside-down triangle

   b) Diamond

   c) Octagon

Chapter 7: California DMV Permit Practice Test 4 (50)

1. You should maintain a straight ahead position with your wheels until it is safe to turn left. Why?

    a) **If a car hits you from behind while your wheels are oriented to the left, you risk being thrown into the path of oncoming traffic.**

    b) The wheels will already be turning in the proper way if you change your mind.

    c) Deactivating your anti-lock system is simpler.

2. You should really be driving as you merge onto the motorway:

    a) The freeways posted maximum speed restriction.

    b) 10 to 15 MPH more slowly than the interstate traffic.

    c) **At or close to the exact same speed as the freeway's traffic.**

3. What it says:

    a) Steps for pedestrians up ahead.

    b) Pedestrians must give way to vehicles up ahead.

    c) **Up ahead, a pedestrian crossing.**

4. Who is most in danger?

    a) Drivers who are late for work.

    b) **Long-distance drivers who don't stop for breaks.**

    c) Drivers with experience.

5. Drivers are required to abide by crossing guard instructions:

    a) Just during the school day.

    b) Just outside a school.

    c) **All the time.**

6. When do you have to relinquish your legal right of way?

a) Frequently, even at intersections under control.

b) When it aids in collision avoidance.

c) Never, as other drivers become confused.

7. Cycling in the dark requires:

   a) A front bulb that can be seen from 100 feet away and that emits yellow light.

   b) A rear red reflector that can be seen from 500 feet away.

   c) A white reflector on the helmet of the rider.

8. Driving close to a road repair zone requires you to:

   a) Pass carefully through the construction area and stay focused.

   b) As you pass, slow down to observe the work.

   c) Decrease the distance you follow.

9. Make sure the following when you drive on the highway:

   a) You change lanes before your directional signal sounds.

   b) Must announce every lane change.

   c) When you change lanes, you pass cars behind you.

10. When there aren't any crosswalks or signals for pedestrians, pedestrians:

    a) Should wait till there is no traffic before crossing.

    b) Have priority over bicycles but not over motor vehicles.

    c) Should move off the curb as quickly as possible to prevent getting struck.

11. What do the blue traffic signs mean?

    a) Road user services are shown by blue.

    b) A regulatory sign has a blue background.

    c) They provide directional data.

12. Separating lines in yellow

    a) A two-way road with traffic travelling in the opposing directions.

    b) laned traffic on one-way streets.

    c) From ordinary traffic lanes, all carpool lanes.

13. Drivers can require additional room for the front of their car:

    a) Whether towing a trailer or carrying a hefty load.

    b) When riding behind motorcycles.

c) The aforementioned.

14. Trees obstruct your view to the side for the final 100 feet before crossing as you approach a junction. When considering the intersection:

   a) "Blocked"

   b) "Open"

   c) "Blind"

15. When cars encounter this road sign, they must:

   a) Turn around right away.

   b) Phone the police and come to a complete halt.

   c) Don't go around this sign.

16. the most slick surfaces are roads:

   a) After a hours or more of rain had fallen.

   b) The first downpour following a dry spell.

   c) For the initial two hours of a downpour.

17. When driving beside a light rail car:

   a) They travel slowly and loudly, like freight trains.

   b) Always move carefully to the right when passing a light rail vehicle.

   c) Never make a turn in front of a light rail car that is coming.

18. When a red light at a crossing flashes, it means:

   a) Before entering, pause.

   b) Be cautious when entering.

   c) Wait for the green light and then stop.

19. It is not advisable to:

   a) Let room between your car and the one in front of it.

b) Observe your surroundings.

c) **Follow the vehicle ahead very narrowly.**

20. Alcohol:

    a) Enhances your response time.

    b) Makes it simpler to choose correctly.

    c) **Makes you less conscious of how your driving skills are changing.**

21. The image depicts a _____ sign.

    a) Abrupt bend

    b) No left turn

    c) **No U-turn**

22. Does a car ready to enter a rotary or traffic circle have the right-of-way over cars already in the circle?

    a) **No, the vehicles in the circle already there have the right-of-way.**

    b) Absolutely, but only when they are coming from the right lane into the rotary.

    c) Yes.

23. Which of the below roads is more likely to be slick on chilly, rainy days?

    a) **Roads on overpasses and bridges.**

    b) Roads close to hills' summits.

    c) Rural roads.

71

24. What this sign says

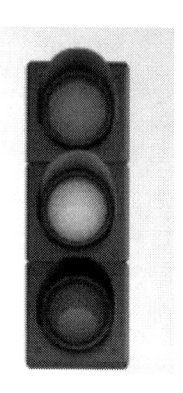

- a) Continue moving at your present rate
- b) You must halt up front.
- c) Speeding is prohibited.
- **d) There is a traffic signal ahead.**

25. A hazard is created when a car "cuts" next to you suddenly. Which of them should you carry out first?

- a) Honk and forcefully press the brake.
- b) Enter the lane next to you with a turn.
- **c) Remove your foot off the gas.**

26. At a junction, you're at a standstill. The stop sign suddenly became green. Should you leave right away?

- a) Sure, or you risk getting a ticket for causing congestion.
- b) No, since you have to wait five seconds before moving on.
- **c) Sure, however you must give way to any parked cars or pedestrians.**

27. Risk indicators include:

- a) Rectangular
- b) Triangular
- **c) Diamond-shaped.**

28. What action should you take if you notice smoke coming from the hood?

- a) After making a call to the fire department, park your car and pull off the road.
- b) Attempt to put out the fire on your own.

c) Parking your car requires pulling off the road. Get out of the car, turn off the ignition, and dial the fire department.

29. You're getting set to turn to the right. You ought to:

   a) Give a signal and make a quick turn.

   b) Stop before moving into the right lane and give way to all oncoming cars.

   c) If you need to, slow down or halt before making the turn.

30. The street you are on is one-way. A left turn into a different one-way street is only permitted if:

   a) The street's traffic shifts to the right.

   b) The turn is permitted by a sign.

   c) The street's traffic shifts to the left.

31. When you enter another lane or change lanes, you:

   a) Possess the right of way.

   b) Should first halt and look out for oncoming vehicles.

   c) Need a traffic gap of at least four seconds.

32. Drivers should: If there is a large puddle in the road ahead

   a) If possible, they should veer their car around the water.

   b) Once they pass through the water, they change to neutral.

   c) They keep moving forward and pass through the water.

33. What actions should you take if your headlights fail unexpectedly?

   a) Lift your foot off the gas and softly use the brakes.

   b) As soon as you can, brake and turn on your emergency lights.

   c) Utilize your directional signals, parking lights, and emergency lights.

34. Driving more slowly than the flow of traffic will most likely cause you to:

   a) Get a ticket for obstructing traffic.

   b) Narrow the traffic flow.

   c) Encourage other drivers to follow suit.

35. To discharge cargo, a big vehicle is backing up. You ought to:

   a) Try to follow closely.

b) **Wait patiently until the big car has finished its backup maneuver.**

c) Wait in one of the blind locations.

36. As the signal light on your vehicle becomes green, a pedestrian is standing in the centre of the road. You ought to:

   a) If the pedestrian is not in your lane, continue.

   b) **Before moving forward, wait until the pedestrian has crossed in front of you.**

   c) If you have the right-of-way, continue.

37. Before crossing railroad tracks, you should stop:

   a) You have three or more axles on your car.

   b) **When you least expect it, a train could be coming, whether or not you can see it.**

   c) Even if the train tracks aren't running.

38. What does a yellow light that flashes indicate?

   a) **Drivers should proceed cautiously.**

   b) Equivalent to a stop sign

   c) The aforementioned.

39. You should: While driving at night on a roadway with poor lighting

   a) To be more visible to other drivers, keep your instrument lights bright.

   b) If you want to see the cars directly in front of you better, switch on your high beam headlights.

   c) **Drive at a pace that will allow you to stop in the area that your headlights have illuminated.**

40. When approaching a bend or a hill's summit, you should:

   a) Prior to negotiating the curve, make an effort to pass the car in front of you.

   b) Accelerate more quickly.

   c) **Not use the left-hand side of the road to drive.**

41. Before moving back into the right lane after passing a vehicle, you must:

   a) Check the rearview mirror of your car.

   b) Signal.

c) The aforementioned.

42. Drivers should NOT: in the event of skidding

   a) **They press their foot on the throttle pedal.**
   b) Remove their foot from the gas.
   c) If they are about to hit something, gently pump the brakes.

43. There is just one lane in your direction, and frequently the car in front of you will suddenly slow down. In this case, you ought to:

   a) **Increasing the following separation between your car and the opposing one**
   b) To warn other drivers, swiftly flash your headlight.
   c) Pass the car as soon as you can.

44. Parking is indicated by a blue-painted curb:

   a) No more than 15 minutes should be permitted.
   b) In order to pick up or drop off passengers.
   c) **For people with disabilities who have a special plate or placard.**

45. Seat belts are supposed to _____ air bags.

   a) **Work with**
   b) Fix
   c) Replace

46. A person who has a Class C driver's license is permitted to:

   a) **A vehicle with three axles if the gross vehicle weight is under 6,000 pounds.**
   b) Whatever a three-axle vehicle, regardless of weight.
   c) A car towing two trailers

47. This sign informs motorists that:

a) No U-turns are permitted.

b) At the intersection, a left turn is required.

c) They can't turn to the right.

48. Those driving automobiles should:

a) While they may brake differently than conventional motor vehicles, try to pass them.

b) Keep greater room between their car and the curb.

c) Cut back on the required following distance.

49. You strike a parked car but can't locate the driver. How do you proceed?

a) Hold off until the owner comes back.

b) On the parked car, attach a note with your name and address.

c) After you arrive home, contact your insurance provider.

50. You've agreed to submit to a test to determine the amount of alcohol in your blood, breath, or urine:

a) Only if you've had alcohol beforehand.

b) When you are on the road in California.

c) Only when there has been a collision.

Chapter 8: California DMV Permit Practice Test 5 (50)

1. You collided lightly with a parked car while driving, but you can't locate the driver. You have to

   a) Post a note on the car.

   b) Report the collision as soon as possible to the local police department or, in unincorporated areas, the CHP.

   c) The aforementioned.

2. During slick conditions, drivers should:

   a) Arrive at a complete halt.

   b) Greater room should be left in front of their car.

   c) To prevent hydroplaning, they should accelerate.

3. A pedestrian is about to cross your lane ahead without using the crosswalk. You ought to:

   a) When you pass the pedestrian, slow down.

   b) Let the pedestrian cross the street completely before continuing.

   c) Past the pedestrian after making eye contact.

4. Which statement regarding seatbelts and collisions is accurate?

   a) Your chances of survival crashes are decreased because safety belts prevent you from being thrown far enough to safety.

   b) Wearing a safety belt improves your chances of surviving the majority of crashes.

   c) If your car has front and side airbags, there is no need to wear a safety belt.

5. Which medication on this list might impair your capacity for driving?

   a) A treatment for the common cold.

   b) Marijuana.

   c) The aforementioned.

6. Some instances of maintaining glass properly include:

   a) Keeping your windows free of obstructions.

   b) Changing out soiled wiper blades.

   c) The aforementioned.

7. Three lanes are being divided by a huge truck: You intend to overtake the big truck. It's best to decline:

   a) Gently on the left and proceed in front of it.

   b) Fast ahead of it and to the left.

   c) Swiftly to the right and proceed in front of it.

8. Driving defensively entails:

   a) Be aware of other drivers' mistakes.

   b) Not look in your mirrors to the rear.

   c) Assume that a driver will truly stop when they come up to a STOP sign on a side road.

9. Red lights are flashing on a school bus that is stopped in your lane up ahead. You ought to:

   a) While the red lights are flashing, stop.

   b) Pass slowly (to 25 MPH) and carefully.

   c) When you believe every child has off the bus, pause before continuing.

10. A route sign's shape reveals the following:

    a) The permitted speed along that route.

    b) That the path you are taking could be hazardous.

    c) What kind of journey you are taking.

11. What else should you do if the back wheels of your car begin to skid?

    a) Pump the pedal gently if the car has ABS.

    b) In order to move the car, turn the steering wheel in that direction.

    c) If your rear wheels start to drift right, turn left.

12. Your turn to the left is going to happen. The final ___ feet before the turn require continuous signaling.

    a) 50

    b) 100

    c) 75

13. Only the following situations allow for the safe carriage of animals in a pickup truck's bed:

a) The truck's tailgate is closed.

b) The truck bed's sides are at least 18 inches tall.

c) They are securely fastened.

14. The best safety measure you can employ when using a phone while driving is:

    a) Before you answer the phone, check the number.

    b) Use hands-free technology to keep both hands on the wheel.

    c) So that you won't have to take your eyes off the road, keep your phone within easy reach.

15. Which of the aforementioned claims regarding blind spots is accurate?

    a) Looking in your rearview mirrors can allow you to assess your blind zones.

    b) If the car has one exterior mirror on each side, they are gone.

    c) Compared to most passenger cars, large trucks have larger blind areas.

16. It is permitted for two motorcycles to:

    a) On deserted highways, race.

    b) With another car, share the lane.

    c) On a single lane, travel side by side.

17. It takes roughly ___ feet to respond and bring the car to a complete stop at 55 mph.

    a) 400

    b) 200

    c) 100

18. While you're following a: Give yourself more room in front of your car.

    a) Station wagon,

    b) A huge tour bus.

    c) A vehicle for people.

19. Choose the best response. Before reversing lanes, you ought to:

    a) To check for blind spots, glance behind you.

    b) See what's in your rearview mirror.

    c) Look over your shoulder and in your rearview mirror.

20. In order to be safe, motorcycle riders must:

   a) Always have their headlights and taillights on.

   b) Put on authorized helmets.

   c) Turn, lane, and stop signals are used.

21. Keeping a tight distance from another vehicle (tailgating):

   a) Is frequently at blame for rear-end crashes.

   b) Aids in preserving traffic flow.

   c) Improves fuel effectiveness.

22. Ahead on your side of the road is a stopped school bus with flashing red lights. You have to

   a) Slow down to 25 MPH and drive cautiously.

   b) Till the lights stop flashing, halt.

   c) Wait until every child has left the bus before stopping.

23. At the corner, a person using a white cane is about to cross the street. The individual draws his or her cane while taking a step back. You ought to:

   a) Wait for the pedestrian to cross the roadway after stopping your car at least six feet from the crosswalk.

   b) The guy is not prepared to cross the street, therefore proceed across it.

   c) When someone is about to enter a crosswalk, blast your horn to let them know, then wait for them to do so.

24. Legally, one may obstruct an intersection:

   a) In the midst of rush hour.

   b) When the light was green and you approached the junction.

   c) Never under any circumstances.

25. The road is particularly slick when it starts to rain on a hot day:

   a) Throughout the initial several minutes.

   b) Once the rain has stopped.

   c) After several hours of rain have passed.

26. What is the sole method that will effectively lower your BAC?

   a) Avoiding alcohol for a while.

   b) Consuming food before or while drinking.

   c) Consuming coffee

27. You must make a left turn at the intersection as you approach a multilane roundabout. You have to

   a) Choose a lane, then leave it in the one you entered.

   b) Select the left-hand lane, then drive out.

   c) Select the right lane, then take the left lane out.

28. Bicyclists:

   a) Possess the same privileges and obligations as motorized vehicles.

   b) Are allowed to drive alongside motor vehicles.

   c) The aforementioned.

29. The act of parking your car is forbidden:

   a) Within a bike lane.

   b) Three feet or less from a private driveway.

   c) In a crosswalk that isn't designated.

30. You want to make a left turn at the next corner. Grant the following right-of-way:

   a) Waiting for the "walk" signal as they go along the sidewalk.

   b) Advancing vehicles also making a left turn.

   c) All en route automobiles.

31. Which of these constitutes safe driving?

   a) Regularly checking your rearview mirrors.

   b) In the fog, use the high beams.

   c) Focusing on the road in front of your car.

32. Those behind the wheel should:

   a) See what is in their rearview mirror.

   b) Abide by the "three-second rule."

   c) Provide the car in front of them at least 25 feet of space.

33. The following must be done if a vehicle passes you on the left:

a) **Slow down a little and stay to the right.**

b) Go a little faster and stay to the right.

c) Reduce your speed, then make a right turn and halt.

34. Which of the following claims concerning drinking and driving is accurate?

a) It is okay to drive after drinking if you can walk straight.

b) **Drinking impairs judgment, which is essential for safe driving.**

c) Driving is not affected if your blood alcohol level is below the legal limit.

35. Driving rules at crossings with stop lines include:

a) **Stop completely.**

b) Signal oncoming vehicles to halt.

c) Slow down and approach the junction.

36. Driving is permitted in a bike lane:

a) If your speed exceeds 15 mph.

b) **200 feet maximum before making a right turn.**

c) Whenever there aren't any cyclists around.

37. While getting ready to turn left onto a two-way street from a one-way street, you must:

a) Approach the turn from the right side of a single lane or in the right lane.

b) To the left of the centre line of the two-way street, turn in.

c) **Approach the turn from the left side of a single lane or from the left lane.**

38. The "Basic Speed Law" of California states:

a) **Never go faster than what is safe for the road conditions.**

b) On some motorways in California, the top speed limit is 70 MPH.

c) Never exceed the posted speed limit when driving.

39. If you can't accelerate to highway speed because the entrance lane is too narrow, you should:

a) As soon as you can, merge into oncoming traffic.

b) **Once there is a significant space in the flow of traffic, enter the highway and accelerate swiftly.**

c) Head to the next entrance ramp.

40. If the vehicle in front of you stops at a crossing, you ought to:

a) Alternate lanes, look up the road, and pass the stationary cars.

b) Once all pedestrians have crossed, halt and go forward.

c) Pass the car slowly at 10 mph or less.

41. Yellow traffic signs:

a) Caution drivers

b) Help drivers.

c) Drivers must stop completely at the indicated stop line when combined with an octagonal form.

42. The image displays:

a) A sign with doubled speeding fines.

b) A caution sign for trains.

c) A traffic sign that may be reversed.

43. A safety zone is a designated place where people can board or exit trams or buses. Driving through a safety zone is prohibited:

a) Anytime, for any cause.

b) Only if a trolley or bus is present.

c) Only when a trolley or bus is emptying its passengers.

44. The uncontrolled "T" intersection is being approached by two vehicles. The through road has one vehicle, while the terminus of the road has the other. At the crossroads, who has the right-of-way?

a) The car to your right.

b) The first vehicle to arrive.

c) The automobile on the throughway.

45. If you continue to be in a big car's back blind spot:

   a) The large car will stop more slowly.

   b) You can lower your gasoline usage.

   c) You raise the likelihood of a collision.

46. Which style of pavement marking indicates the lane you need to be in when making a turn?

   a) Diamond

   b) Edge line

   c) Arrows

47. You should never leave your car parked within _ feet of a fire station driveway, according to the DMV manual.

   a) 10

   b) 15

   c) 25

48. A four-way stop sign indicates:

   a) The intersection has four stop signs.

   b) The first car to arrive at the crossroads should proceed.

   c) The aforementioned.

49. You are driving on a five-lane freeway in the lane closest to the center divider. You should: to leave the motorway on the right:

   a) To get into the right lane, switch lanes one at a time.

   b) Before starting each lane shift, be cautious.

   c) At once, cautiously cross all lanes.

50. Which of the following assertions concerning huge vehicles is accurate?

   a) They can all stop swiftly because to their air brakes.

   b) Compared to passenger cars, they are more maneuverable.

   c) Compared to passenger cars, they take longer to stop.

Chapter 9: California DMV Permit Practice Test 6 (50)

1. When: You are required to alert the authorities and submit a Report of Traffic Accident Occurring in California (SR 1) to the DMV.

    a) **When two objects collide, someone is hurt or killed.**
    b) For your car, you want to submit a certificate of non-operation.
    c) Due to illegal parking, your car is being towed.

2. When a school bus arrives, you must:

    a) Before the red lights cease flashing, pass the bus.
    b) Shut off the engine.
    c) **None of the aforementioned.**

3. Which of the following is true with young passengers:

    a) The front seat should be reserved for children 1 and older and over 20 pounds.
    b) For kids six years old and older, the front seat is typically the safest spot in the car.
    c) **In automobiles with airbags, infants under one should not sit in the front seat.**

4. Terminus symbols are _____ with _____ letters and symbols.

    a) **Green; white**
    b) Blue; white
    c) White; black

5. Entering a junction is prohibited when

    a) When the light is yellow, you can stop without risk.
    b) **Until the light turns red, you cannot travel the entire distance.**
    c) You didn't stop before the light turned yellow and is now flashing.

6. If water on the road causes your car to start losing traction:

    a) Keep moving at the same pace to get more traction.
    b) To stop your car from slipping, press the brakes firmly.
    c) **Do not slam on the brakes as you slowly reduce speed.**

7. Trucks, unlike passenger vehicles, have blind spots:

    a) Right-hand side.

b) Near the front.

c) Directly behind them

8. Which of the below statements concerning big vehicles is correct:

    a) Due to their massive size, trucks frequently appear to move more slowly.

    b) It is preferable to overtake trucks on the right side and very gently.

    c) Trucks' higher height results in less blind zones for the vehicle.

9. What emergency protocol should you always follow?

    a) Make a police call.

    b) Don't freak out.

    c) Move away.

10. What do this street sign mean?

    a) Area designated for disabled individuals

    b) Hospital services

    c) Federal highway

11. A thudding noise may serve as a warning:

    a) Indicating a tyre blowout is imminent.

    b) Of a bad steering.

    c) Of faulty brakes.

12. The octagonal form is employed:

    a) To alert drivers to any dangers that may be present on the route.

    b) Particularly for stop signs.

    c) When it comes to stoplights and railway advance warning signs.

13. What will you do before backing out of a driveway if kids are nearby?

a) Put your mirrors to use.

b) Check for kids in your back window.

c) Check behind car after getting out.

14. What it says:

    a) Road is hazardous when wet. Drive carefully.

    b) Ahead is a winding road. Drive carefully.

    c) The route will then turn right before turning left.

15. If an approaching vehicle's headlights cause you to become temporarily blinded, you should:

    a) Keep your eyes away from the bright lights.

    b) In order to ascertain the location of the other car, swiftly scan the side of the road and then look forward.

    c) The aforementioned.

16. Where do yield signs typically go?

    a) If there isn't a clearly established stop line at an intersection.

    b) Where little roads connect to big roads

    c) Where main roads merge with side roads.

17. You're getting set to turn to the right. You ought to:

    a) On the final 100 feet before turning, signal.

    b) Before making a right turn, always stop.

    c) As you begin your turn, go slowly and give a signal.

18. When is hand-over-hand steering appropriate?

    a) When making quick right turns.

    b) When parked.

    c) The aforementioned.

19. Although you can't see the emergency vehicle, you can hear the siren nearby. How do you behave?

   a) Unless you're certain the emergency vehicle is coming your way, keep driving.

   b) When you are certain that the emergency vehicle is not approaching you, pull over to the right side of the road and stop.

   c) Stop right away, then turn on your emergency flashers.

20. Passing a bike in a congested lane of traffic when a car is coming from behind:

   a) Wait for the approaching car to pass the rider.

   b) Honk your horn before passing the bicycle.

   c) Before passing the bike, slow down and let the car pass.

21. How does a limit sign for speeds look like?

   a) Round

   b) Pentagon

   c) Vertical rectangle

22. Law enforcement will need you to produce proof of insurance:

   a) If you are pulled over for a ticket or involved in an accident.

   b) Solely in the event of a collision.

   c) Only if you are caught and issued a ticket

23. You wish to pass the car in front of you as you are travelling at 55 MPH on a two-lane highway with one lane in each direction. To successfully pass, you must:

   a) Wait until the lanes are divided by solid double-yellow lines.

   b) Have enough space between you and the oncoming traffic.

   c) You should accelerate to at least 60 mph.

24. Every interstate carpool lane is legal for you to use if and only if:

   a) Heavy traffic has stopped all other lanes.

   b) You transport the bare minimum of passengers indicated on the sign.

   c) That happens between 7 p.m. and 7 a.m.

25. Drivers should ride at least _____ from the air bag cover in order to eliminate or lessen air bag risk.

a) 2 inches

b) 20 inches

c) 10 inches

26. Red light left turns are permitted:

    a) Never.

    b) Entering a one-way street from another one.

    c) If the path is clear, stop after halting at junctions.

27. Drivers who notice a crossbuck sign:

    a) Must slow down and watch for the flashing red lights.

    b) Are obligated to give way to trains under the law.

    c) Always needs to cease completely.

28. it's very misty out there. According to the Basic Speed Law, if you are travelling at 45 mph in a 55 mph zone, the following may result in a ticket:

    a) Driving "too quickly" for the circumstances.

    b) Travelling less quickly than the Basic Speed Limit.

    c) Going too slowly.

29. You are travelling at 65 mph on a motorway. Heavy traffic is going at a 35 mph speed. Most likely, the ideal speed for your car is:

    a) 35 mph

    b) 30 mph

    c) 65 mph

30. With a pentagonal symbol, you may say:

    a) Crossings at schools.

    b) No zones for passing.

    c) Possible dangers on the roads.

31. Only from a certain direction can you turn left on a red light:

    a) Onto a one-way street from a two-way street

    b) From a one-way to a two-way roadway.

    c) Onto a one-way street from another one.

32. When stopping at a junction, take a moment to look:

a) **Left, right, then left once again.**

b) Both to the left and forward.

c) Right and left.

33. When a car is 300 feet away or coming from behind you, you should dim your lights:

a) You've already made it.

b) Coming towards you from behind.

c) **You're coming up from behind.**

34. When a traffic light at an intersection is malfunctioning, drivers should:

a) Before proceeding through the intersection, halt and give way to any oncoming traffic.

b) **When it is safe to continue, come to a complete halt.**

c) If required, reduce speed or halt.

35. If you know you'll block the junction when the lights turn red, you shouldn't start crossing an intersection:

a) Unless you approached the junction while the signal was green.

b) **Whatever the circumstances.**

c) Unless you approached the junction while the signal was yellow.

36. What do a school bus' flashing red lights mean?

a) A stop is imminent for the bus.

b) **The bus stops so that passengers can board or disembark.**

c) Both directions of approaching traffic are allowed to move forward.

37. What should you do as soon as your wheels veer off the pavement?

a) Reverse the direction of the wheel.

b) To alert other drivers, pull over to the right and honk your horn.

c) **Lift your foot off the gas and softly use the brakes.**

38. It is forbidden to block a junction during rush hour:

a) **No matter what, even if your light is green.**

b) Unless you approached the junction while the signal was green.

c) Unless you have a green light or the right-of-way.

39. A yellow light that is flashing denotes:

    a) The green light will shortly turn to red.

    b) At the intersection, give other traffic the right-of-way.

    c) Drive carefully.

40. All passengers under the age of eight must be restrained in a child safety seat unless:

    a) There is no available kid passenger restraint system.

    b) Must wear a safety belt and are 4 feet, 9 inches or taller.

    c) The kid passenger restraint system is not used by them.

41. With both lights and a siren, an emergency vehicle might be surprising. Why?

    a) Drivers of emergency vehicles are not required to exercise caution.

    b) Legally, the driver may go through red lights.

    c) When it is safe to do so, emergency vehicles must travel faster than the posted speed limit.

42. A red-painted curb is:

    a) No standing, parking, or stopping.

    b) Stop no longer than the posted amount of time to load or unload cargo or people.

    c) Don't stop more than is necessary to pick up or drop off passengers.

43. _____ if your car is air bag-equipped.

    a) Always buckle up when you're in a car.

    b) The wearing of seatbelts is not required.

    c) Never wear a seatbelt.

44. What makes nighttime driving more challenging than daytime driving?

    a) Diminished visibility

    b) Maintaining a safe distance.

    c) The legislation requires that headlights be used.

45. Ahead, on the right shoulder of the road, a car is stopped with its hazard lights on. You ought to:

    a) Pass slowly and with great caution.

b) Speed up and veer to the left to change lanes.

c) To view what has transpired, move onto the right shoulder of the road.

46. Drivers can make a U-turn unless specifically banned by a sign:

    a) A one-way street at an intersection.

    b) Ahead of a school.

    c) At an intersection where the light is green.

47. While being stopped by law enforcement, you ought to:

    a) Stepping out of your car to recognize the officer's presence is required.

    b) Enter the middle median, then stop.

    c) Before relocating your car to the right shoulder of the road, turn on your right turn signal.

48. When motorists encounter a "Wrong Way" sign:

    a) To go to the next intersection, they must pass this sign while driving.

    b) On an exit ramp for a motorway, they are travelling the opposite way.

    c) Except in an emergency, they cannot leave the pavement.

49. When one of the following conditions is met, it is OK for them to ride in the pickup truck's back:

    a) The pickup bed's sides are at least 24 inches tall.

    b) A camper shell is positioned on the pickup's back.

    c) Employing appropriate safety belts and securing seats.

50. Normally, traffic lights are _____ from the top to the bottom or from left to right.

    a) red, yellow and green

    b) green, yellow and red

    c) red, green and yellow

Chapter 10: California DMV Permit Practice Test 7 (50)

1. It could be challenging to determine a motorcycle's speed because:

       a) **Your field of vision is less obstructed by motorcycles.**

       b) Motorcycles frequently downshift to slow down.

       c) Many motorcycle riders fail to turn on their brake lights.

2. You are travelling at 65 mph on a motorway. At 70 mph, the traffic is moving. You're allowed to drive:

       a) Somewhere between 65 and 70 mph.

       b) To keep up with the flow of traffic, travel at 70 mph or faster.

       c) **Not exceeding 65 mph.**

3. What do orange traffic indicators indicate?

       a) Alerting people to school, pedestrian, and bicycle traffic.

       b) **Warning about construction and maintenance.**

       c) Yield.

4. What are the advantages of having a gap cushion around your car?

       a) To shield you from harm in the event of a collision, it inflates.

       b) **You have time to retaliate if a different driver makes a mistake.**

       c) In order to improve traffic flow, other drivers may "cut" in front of you.

5. If the gas pedal on your car gets stuck, you should:

       a) Take your foot off the gas and slowly apply the brakes.

       b) In the event that your car has power steering, shut the ignition off.

       c) **Try to release the shoe by hooking it beneath the pedal. If not, put your car in neutral, apply the brakes to slow it down, and pull off the road.**

6. When operating a vehicle in two-way traffic on a multi-lane street:

       a) **Drive either in front of or behind the other cars.**

       b) Driving in the lane closest to the center line is the safest option.

       c) So that the drivers of the other vehicles can see you, drive next to them.

7. Your emergency flashers should always be on when:

   a) Driving through dense fog.

   b) Your car has stopped working on the road.

   c) You halt close to a red-painted curb.

8. You have to turn left as you enter a public road from a private road. You must give way to:

   a) Cars coming from the left.

   b) Cars coming in from the right.

   c) Cars travelling in both directions.

9. Aim of this sign

   a) Ahead is four-lane traffic

   b) Highway divided ahead

   c) Ahead is two-way traffic

   d) Upcoming intersection

10. You should do the following to stop driving aggressively:

    a) Make adjustments to your schedule to drive when there is less traffic on the roadway.

    b) Stream some hard metal.

    c) To get where you're going on time, give yourself adequate time to travel.

11. There are no warning signs at the railroad crossing, and you can't see 400 feet down the rails in one way as you approach. The permitted speed is:

    a) 25 mph

b) 20 mph

c) 15 mph

12. On a road with one lane for each direction, if you keep passing other cars you will:

    a) Reduce the likelihood that a crash will happen because of a traffic jam.

    b) Travel considerably safer to your destination.

    c) Raise the likelihood of being in an accident.

13. When a vehicle enters or leaves a roundabout:

    a) Must reduce speed.

    b) Has to stop for all traffic.

    c) Possess the right of way.

14. Which statement regarding railroad crossings is accurate?

    a) Trains are unable to veer aside. On the railroad rails, never stop.

    b) Red lights that flash mean you need to halt and wait.

    c) The aforementioned.

15. On a motorway, you must: If you notice orange construction cones or signage, you must:

    a) The lane is going to end up there, so make a U-turn.

    b) Be ready for employees and machinery up ahead.

    c) While changing lanes, keep the same speed.

16. You may turn from any roadway with two tracks in your direction when making a right turn, including:

    a) The lane that is closest to the middle of the street.

    b) The lane that is closest to the road's edge or curb.

    c) Depending on incoming traffic, either lane.

17. How should you do if you encounter a sign that reads "Wrong Way"?

    a) Call the police and come to a complete halt.

    b) Quickly perform a U-turn.

    c) As you reach the side of the road, stop. Back out or turn around when it's safe to do so, and then take the same route back.

18. It is dark. High beams from a car coming at you make it difficult to see the road in front of you. You ought to:

   a) In your lane, keep your eyes straight ahead.

   b) Observe the right side of your lane as you travel forward.

   c) Observe the left side of your lane as you travel forward.

19. Whose job is it to know whether your prescription affects your ability to drive?

   a) Yours

   b) Your Doctor

   c) Your pharmacist's

20. Parking is permitted according to this blue sign:

   a) For people with disabilities who lack a specific plate or placard.

   b) Only for wheelchair users.

   c) Only for people with disabilities who have a specific plate or placard.

21. To overtake another vehicle, you may cross a double yellow line if the yellow line is near to:

   a) The line on your side of the street is broken.

   b) A solid line runs along the other side of the street.

   c) The line is broken on the opposite side of the street.

22. it's necessary to slow down when driving:

   a) When the terrain is slick.

   b) At railroad overpasses.

   c) The other responses are accurate.

23. If a threatening driver approaches you, you should:

96

a) Keep your composure and ease.

b) Consider making a safe exit.

c) The aforementioned.

24. Two solid yellow lines in the middle of the road should not be crossed to:

   a) Turn left here.

   b) Go through a gated driveway.

   c) Overtake other cars.

25. For the majority of California's roadways, the top speed limit is:

   a) 65 mph

   b) 70 mph

   c) 55 mph

26. It is okay to get back into your lane after passing another car if you:

   a) Have passed the front bumper of the opposing vehicle.

   b) You are unable to see the car immediately to your right.

   c) In the rearview mirror, you can see the car's headlights.

27. When do you need to turn on your headlights?

   a) From one hour prior to sunset until one hour following sunrise.

   b) Whenever you can't see more than two miles in front of you.

   c) Whenever you experience difficulty seeing or being noticed by others.

28. How do you rotate your front tires to park next to a curb while going downhill?

   a) Keep clear of the curb

   b) In line with the curb.

   c) Toward the curb

29. When is it acceptable to lawfully bypass or enter a railroad crossing gate?

   a) Never under any circumstances.

   b) While none of the danger lights are blinking.

   c) When both directions are visible clearly.

30. Signage with a diamond shape:

a) Are used to alert drivers to dangers on the road.

b) Usually provide drivers direction.

c) Represent no pass zones.

31. There is a Basic Speed Law in California, which provides that:

    a) Drivers must adhere to the basic (standard) speed limit at all times.

    b) Never let the weather or the state of the roads dictate how fast you drive.

    c) Drivers are never allowed to go faster than is secure under the current traffic and weather circumstances.

32. This is a sign of

    a) Road tightens, right lane finishes

    b) Separated highway ahead

    c) Hill onward

    d) Truck overpass

33. What form do a warning sign take?

    a) Pennant

    b) Triangle

    c) Diamond

34. If an approaching car doesn't lower its high lights at night, look:

    a) Near the middle of the street.

    b) The right shoulder of the road.

    c) Going forward in your lane.

35. If a person is crossing the street in the midst of a block:

    a) The right-of-way belongs to the pedestrian.

b) **The right-of-way belongs to the pedestrian.**

c) Despite having the right-of-way, drivers are required by law to ensure the safety of pedestrians.

36. Controlling symbols are _____ rectangles with _____ letters or signs.

    a) Yellow; black

    b) **White; black**

    c) Green; white

37. The speed boundary for a school region where kids are present is _____, unless otherwise posted.

    a) 20 mph

    b) 15 mph

    c) **25 mph**

38. In a moving vehicle, you must always wear your seatbelt:

    a) **And if you don't, you'll get a penalty for driving recklessly.**

    b) Unless you are a camper or pickup truck on the rear.

    c) Unless the car was created prior to 1975.

39. You should: To help an officer perform a traffic stop:

    a) **To alert other drivers that there is a danger up ahead, turn on your emergency flashers.**

    b) Attempt to plough into the police car.

    c) Until the patrol car has turned off its emergency lights, accelerate

40. When the signal light becomes yellow, you are travelling at the allowed speed as you approach a junction. You ought to:

    a) **If you can safely do so, halt before going through the intersection.**

    b) Slow down and drive straight through the junction.

    c) Prior to the light turning red, move quickly through the junction.

41. When a flashing yellow signal light appears at a junction, you ought to:

    a) **Pass cautiously and move more slowly.**

    b) Keep driving at the same pace while keeping an eye out for other cars.

    c) Cross the junction only after stopping.

42. You should really be driving: when transferring to a motorway

   a) At the permitted speed on a motorway.

   b) At a speed that is comparable to that of highway traffic.

   c) Slower than the traffic on the motorway.

43. During driving, you should always keep an eye out for:

   a) The area around you.

   b) Observe only the cars in front of you.

   c) Always maintain a forward-facing gaze.

44. Your front wheels ought to be the following while parking uphill on a two-way street without a curb:

   a) Made a left turn (toward the street).

   b) Parallel to the road.

   c) Made a right turn (away from the street).

45. This sign indicates that

   a) On this road, turns are not permitted.

   b) Ahead, the road becomes more congested.

   c) There are several turns up ahead.

   d) When wet, the road could be treacherous.

46. You ought to activate your windscreen wipers on wet, icy, or foggy days and:

   a) When driving on wet pavement, apply the brakes.

   b) Arrive at a complete halt.

   c) So that other cars can see you, turn on your headlights.

47. This is a sign of

   a) Trucks below 18,000 lbs. allowable

   b) Hills ahead

   c) Truck halt ahead

   d) None of Above

48. In order to lessen the chance of slipping on slick surfaces, it is suggested that you:

   a) Be close to the car in front of you and be prepared to stop suddenly.

   b) After beginning to descend a steep hill, change into a lower gear.

   c) Before approaching curves and intersections, slow down.

49. Use of the seat belt is required:

   a) Unless you're driving a car that was made before 1978.

   b) And if you don't, you'll get a penalty for driving recklessly.

   c) Except while travelling in a limousine.

50. This crimson and white symbol advises you to:

   a) Before continuing, halt and inspect the traffic in both directions.

   b) Maintain a constant speed and scan for oncoming vehicles.

   c) Give the traffic on the route you want to enter or cross the right-of-way.

Chapter 11: California DMV Permit Practice Test 8 (50)

1. This crimson and white symbol advises you to:

a) Before continuing, halt and inspect the traffic in both directions.

b) Maintain a constant speed and scan for oncoming vehicles.

c) Give the traffic on the route you want to enter or cross the right-of-way.

2. At junctions where two or more vehicles stop simultaneously at STOP signs and are at an angle:

a) Drivers on the right and left must make way for one another.

b) The motorist on the left must let the motorist on the right go.

c) Right-of-way belongs to the driver who is running late for work.

3. This is a sign of

a) Children having fun

b) There are bicycle rentals available here.

c) Park entrance is in front; be aware of vehicles

d) Road crosses the bike path; be aware of riders

4. Most roadway work zones employ the following signs:

102

a) **Form of a diamond.**
b) Round.
c) Rectangular in form.

5. In your direction, there are two lanes of traffic. The driver in front of you wants to drive more quickly because there are numerous vehicles passing them on the right as you are travelling in the left lane. You ought to:

   a) Maintain your present speed and stay in your lane.
   b) To allow the other motorist to pass, move into the left shoulder.
   c) **When it's safe to do so, move over into the right lane.**

6. Instructions given by road traffic officers' _____ signs, signals or roadway markings.

   a) Necessity obey
   b) Are fewer important than
   c) **Take precedence over**

7. The following road markers identify picturesque regions and parks:

   a) Green and white.
   b) Black and orange.
   c) **Brown and white.**

8. Cross railroad lines with multiple tracks when at a stop:

   a) Once the train has gone by your road.
   b) Only when other cars start to cross.
   c) **Only once you have unobstructed vision in both directions.**

9. When a vehicle is followed excessively closely, it is referred to as:

   a) Tailgating.
   b) **Close tailing.**
   c) Speed gating.

10. You are typically in a huge truck's blind spot if you:

    a) **Unable to see the truck driver in the side mirror of the truck.**
    b) Drive close to the left front wheel of the big vehicle.
    c) Follow the big truck no closer than ten feet behind it.

11. In a crosswalk-free intersection, who has the right-of-way?

    a) Just pedestrians with the green "WALK" signal, though.

    b) The right-of-way is always given to pedestrians.

    c) Vehicles, although they should be cautious and slow down.

12. Whatever ought to you do if you don't have ABS and your brakes fail?

    a) To exert more pressure, quickly and forcefully push the brake pedal.

    b) Try to release the shoe by hooking it beneath the pedal.

    c) Set the cruise control.

13. Consistently moving more slowly than other traffic

    a) Is always more secure than exceeding the speed limit in traffic.

    b) Can prevent movement.

    c) Is a sensible method of defensive driving?

14. Along with a driver on your right, you both arrive at an uncontrolled junction and get ready to proceed straight. The person has the right-of-way.

    a) You.

    b) The other driver.

    c) No one.

15. You must give an emergency vehicle the right-of-way by

    a) Driving slowly till it passes in the right lane.

    b) Even if you are in an intersection, stop right away.

    c) Driving as close as you could to the right side of the road, then stopping.

16. A police car is pursuing you with flashing lights and blaring sirens. You veer off course after being admonished to stop. One individual suffers a severe injury while being chased. You are liable for:

    a) Attending a class on anger control.

    b) Up to seven years' jail in a state prison.

    c) No less than $5,000 in penalties.

17. Two parallel sets of strong double yellow lines, at least two feet apart:

   a) Cannot be crossed at any time.

   b) On roadways having two or more lanes going in the same direction, separate traffic lanes.

   c) Only when it is secure to do so, may it be crossed to do a U-turn.

18. There isn't a stop line at a stop sign, so you must stop:

   a) After you have reached the crossing.

   b) Prior to using the crossing.

   c) Prior to approaching the intersection.

19. When a designated disability parking space is surrounded by a crosshatched area, it means:

   a) Stop only for as long as is indicated to load or discharge passengers.

   b) Park for a brief period.

   c) Having no parking

20. If the bottle is one of the following types, you may drive after having opened it:

   a) Within the glove box.

   b) The trunk

   c) Beneath the front seat.

21. It might be challenging to be able to be seen at sunrise or sunset, or in the rain or snow. Turning is an effective way to signal other drivers that you are there:

   a) The instrument panel's lights are on.

   b) The parking light.

   c) At the headlights.

22. What actions should you take if your steering fails?

   a) Not to worry. To let other cars know you are having car trouble, turn on your emergency lights. Drive the vehicle to a halt gradually while moving to the side of the road.

   b) To increase pressure, repeatedly press the gas pedal.

   c) Get off the road right away.

23. Never take U turn from:

    a) The portion of the left lane closest to the middle of the road.

    b) Your current lane.

    c) Lane to the right.

24. When an edge line bends towards the middle of the road, it means:

    a) Up ahead is a constrained bridge.

    b) Ahead, the road gets narrower.

    c) Right turn is required.

25. When turning left onto a two-way street from a one-way street, you must:

    a) To the left of the centre line of the two-way street, turn in.

    b) Turn around and enter the two-way street.

    c) To the right of the middle line of the two-way street, enter.

26. For optimal road conditions, the top speed limit is:

    a) The speed limit.

    b) The velocity of other vehicles moving in the same direction as you.

    c) The forward-moving vehicles' speed.

27. When a law enforcement official sees one of your passenger is not buckled in, they issue a ticket. Which statement is accurate?

    a) No matter how old they are, your passenger will get a ticket.

    b) You and your travel companion will both be issued a ticket.

    c) If the passenger is under the age of 16, you could be given a ticket.

28. This is a sign of

a) First Aid Location

b) Crossroad

c) Rail Road Crossing

d) Church

29. You recently sold your car. The DMV must be notified within ___ days.

a) 10

b) 15

c) 5

30. What does it signify if an incoming car flashes lights at you while there is a time with poor visibility?

a) It was hard to see your car. Your headlights need to be on.

b) You have excessively bright headlights. You ought to mute them.

c) You have excessively bright headlights. Instead, you ought to use parking lights.

31. The street you are on is one-way. You can take a left turn onto a different one-way street:

a) If the direction of the street's traffic is to the right.

b) Only if the turn is permitted by a sign.

c) If the flow of traffic on the street is to the left.

32. It is very important to check behind you before you:

a) Bring down your speed.

b) Alternate lanes.

c) The aforementioned.

33. Cyclists in traffic lanes require extra caution since they:

    a) Have the right-of-way in most cases.

    b) Rider must face incoming traffic.

    c) May be concealed in your blind zones.

34. At a railway crossing, your automobile stalls on the tracks, putting you in danger of being hit by a train. Once you and your passengers have exited the vehicle, you should:

    a) Run towards the direction of the train while avoiding the tracks.

    b) Go around the tracks.

    c) Send a stop-sign to the train.

35. What do alert signs indicate?

    a) The area where there is a specific regulation is coming into view for drivers.

    b) Threat ahead.

    c) The aforementioned.

36. Which statement regarding other drivers is accurate?

    a) Always respect traffic signals and signs as a driver.

    b) While employing turn signals, drivers always make the specified turn.

    c) Never presume that other drivers will yield to you.

37. This sign is used to advise motorists of

    a) Future intersections

b) Building of roads

c) Road turns ahead.

d) Lane changes in the road

38. A car cannot be passed on the left by a driver if

   a) Before the center line transforms from a broken line to a solid one, they cannot return safely to the right lane.

   b) On a two-way road, they approach a hilltop but are unable to look over it.

   c) The aforementioned.

39. Which of the following is true when operating a vehicle while taking medication?

   a) As long as they are recommended by a doctor, medicines are secure to be taken whenever.

   b) The majority of cold remedies have a sedative effect.

   c) If taken as directed, over-the-counter drugs cannot affect one's ability to drive.

40. You should never leave your car parked within _____ feet of a railroad track, according to the DMV rulebook.

   a) 10

   b) 15

   c) 7 ½

41. Which one of the following statements is FALSE? Driving close to pedestrians:

   a) A pedestrian is urging you to across the intersection if they make eye contact with you.

   b) Whenever a person crosses the street at a corner, halt.

   c) Avoid driving on sidewalks.

42. _____ have white characters and symbols on blue backgrounds.

   a) The service signs

   b) Danger signals

   c) Directional signs

43. You should: Before exiting your parked car on the street's traffic side,

   a) Keep an eye out for passing cars, bicycles, and motorcycles.

   b) Indicating with your arm that you are getting out of your car.

c) Your left turn signal should be on.

44. If there is no stop sign or signal when you approach a junction, you:

   a) Should be prepared to halt if necessary and should slow down.

   b) Should never proceed across an intersection without first stopping.

   c) Must let all other vehicles have the right-of-way.

45. In all cases, you should drive with your wheels pointed straight ahead.

   a) Parked without a curb just on side of an even road.

   b) Parked on a sloped driveway or hill.

   c) Waiting at a traffic signal to turn left.

46. If there isn't a crosswalk or a limit line, where do you stop your car?

   a) 20 feet prior to the corner.

   b) Just go around the bend.

   c) The intersection.

47. This is a sign of

   a) School crossing

   b) Business region

   c) Stay on the footpath

   d) Crossing not allowed

48. What else should you do if a threatening driver approaches you?

   a) Establish eye contact.

   b) Keep your distance from the aggressive driver's eyes.

   c) More speed is the answer to the belligerent motorist.

49. There is no curb where you wish to park on a two-way street that slopes downward. What direction do your front wheels turn?

    a) They are therefore facing forward.

    b) Left, towards the direction of the road's center.

    c) Right, in the direction of the roadside.

50. Your side mirrors and rearview mirror should be adjusted:

    a) Prior to entering the car.

    b) Just before you take the wheel.

    c) As soon as you begin driving.

Conclusion

To round things off, let's talk about the skills you'll need to have. Every motorist must educate himself on the correct way to park their vehicle. Your ability will be evaluated based on how well you park on an incline and in a perfectly straight drive-in. The extent to which you can come to a complete stop in the middle of the bay, with sufficient room on each end for the driver and the passengers to escape, will be a significant factor in determining how well you perform throughout the exam. It is important to make sure that any vehicle components that can jeopardize other drivers' safety are removed.

When parked on the incline, the vehicle must remain completely still. In some scenarios, there will be tests on going uphill and downhill, with and without a curb. In case you were curious, the answer to your question is no; passing your driver's test in California does not require you to have parallel parking experience. Having the capability to do so, however, is still valuable.

Your prowess behind the wheel will be put to the test in a variety of various ways throughout this game. The capacity to reverse direction in a limited space is tested during a three-point turn (between 20 and 40 feet).

This test requires that you demonstrate that you can successfully execute a 50-foot backup while looking out the rear window. This is one of the prerequisites. Operating vehicles while using rearview cameras or other comparable equipment is dangerous.

The examiner will also check if you utilize your turn signals in the final one hundred feet before entering a new road, parking space, or lane. This is part of the criteria for passing the test. A hand and electrical signal test may be given.

As you get close to a stop sign, you need to know what to do. The examiner will check whether you come to a complete stop before the line or gradually slow down as you get closer to it. Before you get back on the road, you need to ensure that it is secure to start moving again.

In addition to that, you should be aware of how to go cautiously via a crosswalk. You can resume driving after the signal at the intersection changes to green, and all vehicles have passed through it.

Aside from that, your trainer may suggest that you carry out an emergency stop. Your chances of succeeding and receiving full credit will increase significantly if you execute quickly and carefully.

How you react when you come to a crossing is one of the essential components of the test for your driver's license that deals with the safety of the road. Before you can move forward, you need to ensure that it is safe by checking the surrounding area and getting into the correct lane.

Your inspector will also carefully examine how you use the yield right-of-way granted to you. If you have forgotten the rules for using a pedestrian crossing or a traffic roundabout, you should read this again.

Maintaining one's position within a traffic lane is among the most valuable abilities a driver can develop. Your teacher will ensure that you adhere to all of the appropriate safety procedures whenever you are close to other vehicles. It is also recommended that you maintain a secure distance behind them. Before receiving your driver's license, you must begin engaging in defensive driving techniques.

Last but not least, your overall stance. The position of your seat concerning the steering wheel is crucial. Keep your arms closer to your body and your hands where they should always be on the wheel.